Finding America in Numbers

"In *Finding America in Numbers*, Rabbis Michael J. Broyde and Reuven Travis deliver an inspiring and urgently relevant work. Much like Habakkuk, who sought God's voice in a world of violence and division, the authors courageously navigate the challenging narratives of Numbers—stories of rebellion and judgment—to forge powerful links between biblical truths and the core principles of American democracy. For Christian readers like myself, the book is a revelation, making complex theological and legal ideas beautifully accessible. It compellingly argues that Scripture isn't merely a spiritual foundation but a vital guide for civic engagement and moral action. With profound rabbinic wisdom, Broyde and Travis highlight the shared values that underpin both biblical teachings and American democracy. Their powerful message is clear: In our divided times, the Bible's enduring relevance offers a crucial path to restoring unity and understanding. This book is a beacon for anyone seeking light in the chaos."

—**SHELLEY NEESE**, Coordinator, American Christian Leaders for Israel

"A thought-provoking and timely meditation on the importance of fair process for self-governance and on the persistent hope that struggles for equality will lead to a more inclusive 'we.' By reflecting on the evolving leadership style of Moses, *Finding America in Numbers* illustrates why humility and service to the greater good as leadership traits still matter today and invites Americans to embrace a commitment to our collective flourishing anew."

—**WHITTNEY L. BARTH**, Executive Director, Center for the Study of Law and Religion, Emory University

"*Finding America in Numbers* is an original, refreshing, and scholarly examination of the book of Numbers, drawing a surprisingly direct line from its themes to modern America's theory of government. In an era when it is fashionable to divorce modern political and societal discourse from its biblical antecedents, *Finding America in Numbers* is a cogent demonstration of the relevance of the Bible, in general, and the book of Numbers, specifically, to a comprehensive understanding of the underpinnings of our American society. Rabbis Broyde and Travis's eminently readable survey and analysis of biblical and Talmudic sources is an invaluable resource for understanding the foundations of our modern American society."

—**Ilan Feldman**, Rabbi, Congregation Beth Jacob, Atlanta, Georgia

Finding America in Numbers

A Model of Political Leadership for the 21st Century

Michael J. Broyde and Reuven Travis

WIPF & STOCK · Eugene, Oregon

FINDING AMERICA IN NUMBERS
A Model of Political Leadership for the 21st Century

Copyright © 2025 Michael J. Broyde and Reuven Travis. All rights reserved. Except for brief quotations in critical publications or reviews, no part of this book may be reproduced in any manner without prior written permission from the publisher. Write: Permissions, Wipf and Stock Publishers, 199 W. 8th Ave., Suite 3, Eugene, OR 97401.

Wipf & Stock
An Imprint of Wipf and Stock Publishers
199 W. 8th Ave., Suite 3
Eugene, OR 97401

www.wipfandstock.com

PAPERBACK ISBN: 979-8-3852-3308-3
HARDCOVER ISBN: 979-8-3852-3309-0
EBOOK ISBN: 979-8-3852-3310-6

VERSION NUMBER 07/31/25

biblemapper.com was the source of the Kadesh-barnea map.

Commemorating the untimely passing of Rabbi Lord Jonathan Sacks five short years ago. Eminent Chief Rabbi of the United Hebrew Congregations of the Commonwealth, author of over forty books and hundreds of articles, Rabbi Sacks remains a leading expositor of Jewish values to the Western world.

Never again did there arise in Israel a prophet like Moses—
whom the LORD singled out, face to face.

—Deuteronomy 34:10

The great leaders tell the story of the group, but the greatest of leaders,
Moses, taught the group to become a nation of storytellers.

—Rabbi Jonathan Sacks

Rav and Shmuel both say: Fifty measures of understanding were
created in the world,
and all were given to Moses except one, as it is stated:
"Yet you have deprived him of little, of God" (Psalms 8:6).

—Nedarim 38a

Contents

Acknowledgements | ix
About the Authors | xi

Chapter One
Introduction | 1

Chapter Two
Ends Versus Means | 8

Chapter Three
Moses's Backstory | 23

Chapter Four
Moses's Leadership Roles Prior to Korah's Rebellion | 29

Chapter Five
Moses's Leadership Roles After Korah's Rebellion | 74

Chapter Six
America's Founders and the Numbers Narrative | 94

Chapter Seven
A Need to Look Back in Order to Move Forward | 111

Bibliography | 117

Acknowledgements

ALL TRANSLATIONS OF BIBLICAL verses in this book are taken from *Tanakh: A New Translation of the Holy Scriptures according to the Traditional Hebrew Text* which appears on its website unless otherwise indicated. This translation is available in the public domain and with a free public license thanks to Sefaria.

About the Authors

MICHAEL J. BROYDE

RABBI BROYDE IS PROFESSOR of law at Emory University School of Law and the Berman Projects Director at the Center for the Study of Law and Religion at Emory University. In addition, he directs the doctor of juridical science (SJD) program at Emory University. His primary areas of interest are law and religion, Jewish law and ethics, and comparative religious law. In addition to Jewish law, Rabbi Broyde has taught courses in family law, federal courts, alternative dispute resolution, and secured credit and bankruptcy. He received his *juris doctor* from New York University, where his published note appears in the law review. Following law school, he clerked for Judge Leonard I. Garth of the United States Court of Appeals for the Third Circuit. In 2018, Rabbi Broyde won a Fulbright Senior Scholar Fellowship to study religious arbitration in diverse Western democracies. He also teaches advanced Jewish law at Columbia Law School.

Rabbi Broyde was ordained (יורה יורה ידין ידין) as a rabbi by Yeshiva University and was a member (דיין) of the Beth Din of America, the largest Jewish law court in America. He served as director during the 1997–1998 academic year while on leave from Emory. Rabbi Broyde was also the founding rabbi of the Young Israel synagogue in Atlanta, a founder of the Atlanta Torah MiTzion Kollel study program, and a board member of many organizations in Atlanta.

About the Authors

REUVEN TRAVIS

Prior to his career as an educator, Rabbi Travis spent fifteen years as a consultant and as an advertising and marketing executive. There, he worked for large Fortune 500 firms such as Georgia-Pacific and Ogilvy & Mather. He developed strategic business and marketing plans for a variety of consumer-packaged goods and financial services companies. He then changed professions and started his career as an educator. In this role, he has taught a wide range of classes, including courses on Jewish law, Bible, Jewish history, Zionism, the Shoah (Holocaust), Israel advocacy, American history and civics, and African American history.

Rabbi Travis earned his bachelor's degree from Dartmouth College, where he graduated Phi Beta Kappa, with a double major in French literature and political science. He holds an additional master's degree in teaching from Mercer University and a master's degree in Judaic studies from Spertus College. He received his rabbinic ordination in 2006 from Rabbi Michael J. Broyde, dean of the Atlanta Torah MiTzion Kollel, after spending four years studying with members of the Kollel.

In addition to his collaborations with Rabbi Broyde on the books of Genesis and Exodus, Rabbi Travis has published three scholarly works, which examined the books of Job, Numbers, Genesis. He also authored a series of books about the weekly parasha for parents and educators of children in the third, fourth, and fifth grades.

Chapter One

Introduction

THE END JUSTIFIES THE means. It's a phrase we are all familiar with. Whether we agree with its sentiments is another matter.

Niccolò Machiavelli is often credited with coining the phrase, but that's not true.[1] The closest Machiavelli gets to expressing this view is in Chapter XVIII of *The Prince*:

> [M]en judge generally more by the eye than by the hand, because it belongs to everybody to see you, but few come in touch with you. Everyone sees what you appear to be, few really know what you are, and those few dare not oppose themselves to the opinion of the many, who have the majesty of the state to defend them; and in the actions of all men, and especially of princes, which it is not prudent to challenge, one judges by the result. For that reason, let a prince have the credit of conquering and holding his state, the means will always be considered honest, and he will be praised by everybody; because the vulgar are always taken by what a thing seems to be and by what comes of it; and in the world there are only the

---

1. "Political misquotes."

vulgar, for the few find a place there only when the many have no ground to rest on.[2]

It is a stretch to say Machiavelli is arguing here that a person can do anything so long as the result is good or worthwhile. Even Leon Trotsky, one not often cited in America as a source of moral clarity, understood the problems with reading Machiavelli in such a simplistic manner when he wrote: "A means can be justified only by its end. But the end in its turn needs to be justified."[3] Trotsky's observation is both profound and important. In essence, he is suggesting that whether the ends are justified is sometimes measured by the destruction caused by the means.

This tension between means and ends (or as we will describe it throughout this book, between processes and outcomes) is the basis for this, the fourth of five books we plan to write together about the Torah, the Hebrew Bible, the Five Books of Moses. We have undertaken this project with the goal of demonstrating the continued relevance of the Pentateuch, or the Torah as it is referred to in Judaism, for contemporary Americans.

Lest you doubt that many Americans no longer see the Bible as relevant to their lives, consider that it is not often read by secular readers. According to a recent poll, 29 percent of American adults never read the Bible.[4] Among those who claim to have read it, nearly half (48 percent of respondents) said seldom or never, compared to about a third (35 percent) who claim to read it at least once a week.[5]

This is disconcerting to us, for we believe that American society as a whole is stronger and healthier when undergirded by the moral values put forth in the Bible. That our government functions better when politicians and civil servants are seen as people of integrity and not as disingenuous and dishonest.[6] That our lives

---

2. Machiavelli, *The Prince*, chapter XVIII.
3. Trotsky, *Their Morals & Ours*, 34.
4. "Frequency of Reading the Bible."
5. "Religious Landscape Study."
6. According to the Pew Research Center, just 16 percent of the public say they trust the federal government always or most of the time. While trust

Introduction

are enriched when our common values lead us to trust and respect one another. Indeed, our goals are more easily accomplished with the trust of common values. We think the Bible provides a set of common values, a blueprint if you will, for many aspects of American life.

Today, a record-high 50 percent of Americans rate the overall state of moral values in the US as poor, and another 37 percent say it is only fair. A mere 1 percent think the state of moral values is excellent, and only 12 percent think of them as good. These concerns about America's lost moral compass are not limited to the here and now. Many Americans are also mostly pessimistic about the future on the subject: 78 percent say morals are getting worse and just 18 percent say that it is getting better.[7]

As rabbis and educators, we know that the Bible has lessons that are as relevant today as they were when God appeared to Moses and the Jewish people at Mount Sinai. Our challenge has been to show why these lessons are so critical to these difficult times within which we find ourselves today.[8]

Genesis is arguably the best known of the five books of the Pentateuch. Yet, as we noted throughout our previous books, familiarity does not necessarily equate to relevancy. With regards to Genesis, we sought to demonstrate that it continues to speak to its readers as individuals and that it addresses core issues readers often wrestle with in their daily lives.

In contemporary America, there seem to be few hard and fast rules that govern personal encounters and sexual liaisons.

---

has hovered near historic lows for the better part of the last twenty years, today it stands among the lowest levels dating back nearly seven decades. And more Americans have an unfavorable than favorable opinion of the Supreme Court—the first time that has occurred in polling going back to the late 1980s. See "Americans' Dismal Views of the Nation's Politics."

7. Brenan and Willcoxon, "Record-High 50% of Americans Rate U.S."

8. According to a 2022 poll, most Americans believe divisions have gotten worse since the start of 2021 and few see things improving in the coming years. In fact, 62 percent expect an increase in political divisions. More disturbing is that two in five Americans believe a civil war is at least somewhat likely in the next decade. Orth, "Two in Five Americans Say a Civil War."

Consent, so long as it is neither coerced nor forced, dictates all. Astute students of the Bible will see this aspect of our current social milieu reflected in the book of Genesis. Genesis is not a book about laws. There are no "thou shall" or "thou shall not" commandments given over by God to humanity. Instead, its narrative depicts the cultures of its time as operating on personal choices and personal freedoms. And from the first sexual tryst in the Garden of Eden to the attempted seduction of Joseph by the wife of Potiphar, these consensual encounters tend to end badly. The cautionary nature of these tales underscores the continued relevance of Genesis.

In our second work, we proposed what some might consider a radical re-reading of the Exodus narrative. In Exodus, we see that God charges the Jewish people at Sinai to be a kingdom of priests and a holy nation (Exodus 19:6). Nowhere is freedom found in this exhortation because the Jews were not liberated merely to become a free people. God wanted and expected them to evolve into a nation committed to creating a law-abiding society.

In our book, we brought together examples of how and where America's founders understood this and wove this idea into the basic fabric of the democracy they were creating. What has for centuries set America apart from other nations is its synergistic linking between freedom and the law, which, of course, is something that goes to the heart of the Exodus story. It is also something that makes Exodus relevant to Americans as a whole population, not solely to discrete individuals.

In our third book, we advocated for a redirected reading of Leviticus. As compared to Genesis and Exodus, secular readers are likely quite unaware of its contents, and, to the extent that they know a bit about it, they probably perceive it to be a highly ritualistic text that describes an outdated and primitive sacrificial cult. However, a careful reading of Leviticus makes clear that it is about more than animal sacrifice. It is about nation building. Leviticus sets forth a template for establishing large, regularly-scheduled communal gatherings intended to foster national unity and identity among the Jewish people. Seen in this light, Leviticus retains its relevance in the highly polarized state of affairs that define

INTRODUCTION

America today because its lessons could be instrumental in restoring a sense of national unity to our country.

This brings us to the book of Numbers.

The book of Numbers is—at its core—a chronicle of the wanderings of the Jews in the Sinai wilderness for forty years. Those familiar with its narrative recognize the ongoing miracles that defined the Biblical Jew's day-to-day existence, such as manna falling from heaven to sustain them and Miriam's miraculous well that accompanied them as they journeyed from encampment to encampment.[9] Better known are the frequent outbursts of God's anger at the Jewish people. Here are some of the most notable examples:

- After the spies' misleading and at times false report was delivered after their scouting mission to Canaan, God strikes them dead. As for the people, Moses bluntly tells them: "God heard your loud complaint and, becoming angry, vowed: Not one of those involved, this evil generation, shall see the good land that I swore to give to your fathers" (Deuteronomy 1:34–35).

- In the aftermath of Korah's rebellion against Moses's leadership, "the earth opened its mouth and swallowed them up with their households, all Korah's people and all their possessions" (Numbers 16:32). Soon thereafter, a plague swept through the nation, killing 14,700 individuals (Numbers 17:10–15).

- In the Plains of Moab Shittim, where the men "profaned themselves by whoring with the Moabite women" (Numbers 25:1), God became "incensed," (Numbers 25:3) and in His anger, unleashed a plague that killed 24,000 men (Numbers 25:9).

Jews and Christians alike have wrestled with incidents such as these, trying to reconcile them with their vision of a merciful and forgiving God. Many books and commentaries have addressed this issue, but for secular Americans, the answers offered are often irrelevant, especially if one does not believe in God.

9. Talmud Bavli Taanit 9a.

Finding America in Numbers

This is why we believe the relevance to Americans of Numbers lies elsewhere. Americans ought to know that democracy (even those who have grown skeptical of American democracy[10]) is grounded in process and procedure, not outcomes, as we will discuss later in this book. Moses, who first appears to the Jewish people in the book of Exodus as God's prophet, indeed, the greatest of prophets,[11] ultimately steps back from the role. He then acts as King, but comes to realize that this, too, is not the role he desires or what is needed by the Jewish people as this nation of former slaves transforms itself into a society comprised of free men and women.

In the pages that follow, we discuss how and why Moses concludes that the Jewish people, when they enter the land of Israel and become a sovereign nation, do not need an authoritarian king. Rather, they need a model of systematic government built on the notion of a separation of powers that prevents despots and a more distant God. We will also show that America's founders, many of whom were devout students of the Bible, grasped what Moses was doing in the Numbers narrative and wove it into the very fabric of American democracy.[12] This is certainly not the sole lesson to be

---

10. The commitment of the people of the United States to a democratic system, long taken for granted, is now in doubt. A growing body of research has demonstrated their shaky support for democracy when this is understood as support for *concrete* democratic norms or institutions or a preference for pro- versus antidemocratic political candidates. There is, however, considerable evidence now that Americans' commitment to democracy *even in the abstract* is also in decline. As Voeten puts it, "the United States is an example of a country where support for democracy has gone down while alternatives have become more acceptable." See Claassen and Magalhães, "Public Support for Democracy in the United States."

11. "Never again did there arise in Israel a prophet like Moses—whom God singled out, face to face, for the various signs and portents that God sent him to display in the land of Egypt, against Pharaoh and all his courtiers and his whole country, and for all the great might and awesome power that Moses displayed before all Israel" (Deuteronomy 34:10–12).

12. It is worth noting that this, the notion of separation of powers, is also the basic theme of the book of Joshua, a narrative in which God is more distant than in the five books of the Pentateuch. This also helps explain why Joshua was seemingly unconcerned with naming a leader to succeed him, a primary fixation at the end of Moses's life.

INTRODUCTION

learned from Numbers, but it is among the most important lessons that Americans can learn from this book of the Bible.

A FINAL POINT OF INTRODUCTION

This book is at times heavily footnoted, not because the footnotes are essential for following the flow of our arguments. They are not. Rather, they reflect our many years collectively as educators, where we always strove to provide our students with a context for the material we were discussing. The footnotes in this book do precisely that. They generally provide background information to put matters into context. They also define some Hebrew terms and concepts. Whether you read the footnotes or skip them entirely, you will have a better understanding (we hope) when you reach the end of this book of why the book of Numbers is still worthwhile reading for so many Americans.

Chapter Two

Ends Versus Means

LET'S START WITH THE theoretical and then move on to the practical.

Writers and thinkers from antiquity pondered the concept of the end justifying the means, and they seemed to conclude, as do many in our times, that if a goal is morally important enough, any method of getting it is acceptable. For instance, in the Greek tragedy *Electra*, which dates to c. 409 BCE, the playwright Sophocles wrote: "The end excuses any evil." This same notion was later rendered by the Roman poet Ovid in *The Heroides*[1] (c. 10 BCE) as "The result justifies the deed."

Such sentiments were not intended to justify unnecessary cruelty, Instead, they reflected the political philosophy of the times, one that is today called "consequentialism." In the simplest of terms, consequentialism is a doctrine that posits that the morality of an action is to be judged solely by its consequences.[2] To

---

1. A collection of fifteen epistolary poems composed by Ovid in Latin elegiac couplets.

2. The earliest recorded endorsement in colonial America of consequentialism can be found in the diary of the American clergyman and poet Michael Wigglesworth (1631–1705), who wrote: "Anything is acceptable if it leads to a successful result," Morgan, *Diary of Michael Wigglesworth 1653–1657*.

illustrate the point, consider lying. Most people would agree that lying is wrong and that one should refrain from doing so. However, if telling a lie would save the life of another person, consequentialism maintains that it would be the right thing to do.[3]

An underlying tenet of consequentialism centers on the issue of how to define "right" and "wrong," and our thoughts on this topic are very much influenced by the writings of Immanuel Kant (1724—1804). In particular, we are indebted to his discussion of two terms he coined: "autonomy" and "heteronomy."

In articulating these terms, Kant wanted to emphasize the contrast between his approach to ethics and those that had preceded him.[4] A key to this was to distinguish between hypothetical imperatives and categorical imperatives. Kant believed that principles of duty had in prior years been presented as hypothetical imperatives. He thought that such approaches were misguided and argued that moral principles could only be adequately expressed as categorical imperatives.

The difference between the two is this. Hypothetical imperatives compel individuals to act in order to achieve some desirable end. However, if people are indifferent to the results of this imperative, then they would have little if any reason to act upon it. "Thou shall not commit adultery" is an excellent example of a hypothetical moral imperative. It is undergirded by a desire to please God and avoid punishment in the afterlife. It also carries with it the very practical values of betrayal and loyalty. For those who do not believe in God or in the afterlife, this moral imperative provides no reason for not committing adultery. In contrast, a categorical imperative would simply hold that adultery is wrong. From this perspective, there are no consequences, now or in the future, for one's categorical conclusion that adultery is wrong.[5]

Kant thought that ethical principles had been conceived historically as hypothetical imperatives. What he suggested instead was that the commands of morality are given categorically by each

3. "Consequentialism."
4. Johnson and Cureton, "Kant's Moral Philosophy."
5. Johnson and Cureton, "Kant's Moral Philosophy."

rational agent to themselves, and that is why individuals obey these commands. Thus, the Kantian system of autonomy and heteronomy makes it difficult to accept or reject absolutely the idea that the end justifies the means. Such a calculation can and likely will vary from person to person.

Another philosophical approach to answering whether or not the end can and perhaps should justify the means involves "Utilitarianism." Utilitarianism is one of the most powerful and persuasive approaches to normative ethics in the history of philosophy. Though not fully articulated until the nineteenth century, proto-utilitarian positions can be discerned throughout the history of ethical theory.[6]

Simply put, utilitarianism posits that the morally right action is the action that produces the most good. Two of its biggest proponents, Jeremy Bentham (1748–1832) and John Stuart Mill (1806–1873), thought that the moral value of an act was determined by the pleasure it produced, although Bentham considered only the quantity of pleasure while Mill considered both quantity and quality of pleasure.[7]

As we will soon discuss, both consequentialism and utilitarianism are at odds with Judaism's attitude towards ends and means. Nonetheless, these two philosophical perspectives are applicable to real-life situations where ends and means are frequently debated.

Take, for example, business ethics. In America, most businesses exist for a very simple reason: to make money. Indeed, corporations today operate according to a model of corporate governance known as "shareholder primacy." This theory claims that the purpose of a corporation is to generate returns for shareholders and that decision-making should be focused on a singular goal: maximizing shareholder value. While one might hope and expect that with corporate rights come societal responsibilities, the rules of corporate America do not guarantee that firms advance the

---

6. Driver, "History of Utilitarianism."

7. In a sense, both Bentham and Mill were Epicureans in that they were hedonists about value. Driver, "History of Utilitarianism."

ENDS VERSUS MEANS

public interest.[8] Frequently, businesses, especially large corporations, opt to pursue their ends by any means necessary. If you doubt this is true, simply reflect on the history of the tobacco industry. For decades, "Big Tobacco"[9] ran deceptive campaigns, misled policymakers even when under oath, and funded biased research to help create confusion. For instance, as early as 1954, the tobacco industry paid to publish the "Frank Statement to Cigarette Smokers"[10] in hundreds of US newspapers. It stated that the public's health was the industry's primary concern and promised to make a variety of good-faith changes.[11] None of this was true. Millions of Americans continued to smoke, unaware of the damage it was causing to their bodies. Worse still, regulations were delayed that may have given people the information they needed and which might have protected them from industry predation.[12] The real face of the industry was fully and finally revealed in a landmark 2006 court decision that found that the major US tobacco companies had violated civil racketeering laws (RICO) and engaged in a decades-long conspiracy to deceive the American public about the health effects of smoking and how they marketed to children.[13] In

---

8. Palladino and Karlsson, "Towards Accountable Capitalism."

9. "Big Tobacco" is a name used to refer to the largest companies in the tobacco industry. According to the World Medical Journal, the five largest tobacco companies are: Philip Morris International, British American Tobacco, Imperial Brands, Japan Tobacco International, and China National Tobacco Company.

10. In part, this document stated that "recent reports on experiments with mice have given wide publicity to the theory that cigarette smoking is in some way linked with lung cancer in human beings. Although conducted by doctors of professional standing, these experiments are not regarded as conclusive in the field of cancer research. . . . We accept an interest in people's health as a basic responsibility, paramount to every other consideration in our business. We believe the products we make are not injurious to health. We always have and always will cooperate closely with those whose task it is to safeguard the public health." See "A Frank Statement to Cigarette Smokers."

11. Brownell and Warner, "Perils of Ignoring History."

12. "Decades of Lies Show Tobacco Companies Can't Be Trusted."

13. *United States v. Philip Morris USA Inc.*, 9F. Supp. 2d 1 (D.D.C. 2006).

simplest terms, tobacco companies were found guilty of lying to the American public about the deadly effects of cigarettes and secondhand smoke. They were thus required to run extensive television and newspaper advertising campaigns, at their own expense, admitting the truth about their products.

Despite the facts that are now commonly known, many people continue to smoke, and tobacco continues to kill more than 480,000 Americans annually—more than AIDS, alcohol, car accidents, illegal drugs, murders, and suicides combined.[14] And the industry continues to be extraordinarily profitable.[15] Who's to say that tobacco industry executives don't believe that their financial ends justified the means?

A more recent and more egregious example of the end trumping the means involves Purdue Pharma and its marketing of opioids. In contrast to the immoral and deceitful practices of the tobacco industry, Purdue Pharma, in pursuit of profits,[16] engaged in out-and-out criminal activity.

As part of 2020 plea agreement, Purdue admitted that from May 2007 through at least March 2017, it conspired to defraud the United States by impeding the lawful function of the Drug Enforcement Administration (DEA). Purdue repeatedly reported to the DEA that it maintained an effective anti-diversion program when, in fact, Purdue continued to market its opioid products to more than 100 health care providers that it had good reason to believe were indeed diverting opioids. The misleading information comprised prescription data that included prescriptions written by doctors that Purdue had good reason to believe were engaged in diversion. Purdue also sent misleading information to the DEA to boost Purdue's manufacturing quotas. The conspiracy also involved aiding and abetting violations of the Food, Drug, and

14. "Toll of Tobacco in the United States."

15. In 2024, revenues from all tobacco products—cigarettes, cigars, E-cigarettes, and smoking tobacco, was $107 billion. "Tobacco Products-United States."

16. According to *The Wall Street Journal*, the Sackler family, owners of Purdue Pharma, made as much as $13 billion in profits from the company's sales of opioids. Hopkins and Scurria, "Sacklers Received as Much as $13 Billion."

Ends Versus Means

Cosmetic Act by facilitating the dispensing of its opioid products, including OxyContin, without a legitimate medical purpose, and thus, without lawful prescriptions. Under the terms of the agreement, Purdue agreed to the imposition of the largest penalties ever levied against a pharmaceutical manufacturer, including a criminal fine of $3.544 billion and an additional $2 billion in criminal forfeiture.[17]

To be sure, there are industries that avoid immoral or illegal activities while still placing ends ahead of means and in doing so produce less than desirable outcomes for the general public. Big Oil's continued efforts to thwart emerging "green" technologies is just one example.

Climate change is not new. Scientists have demonstrated that the planet's climate has changed throughout its history, and while some debate the causes, both past and present, one fact is undeniable: global warming is today happening at a rate not seen in the past 10,000 years. Indeed, the evidence that exists in both natural sources (such as ice cores, rocks, and tree rings) and from modern equipment (like satellites and instruments) all show the signs of a changing climate.[18] As the Intergovernmental Panel on Climate Change (IPCC) has noted: "Since systematic scientific assessments began in the 1970s, the influence of human activity on the warming of the climate system has evolved from theory to established fact."[19]

Big Oil cannot plead ignorance. Leaders in the oil and gas industry have understood climate change as human-drive since at least 1982, when Exxon's own researchers helped link carbon emissions and rising temperatures. Despite this, oil companies knowingly made (and continue to make) decisions that contributed to the current crisis.[20] Why? It is because their ends (massive profits) seemingly justify any means.

Despite the pressure oil companies face to invest more money into renewable energy to help fight climate change, there

17. "Opioid Manufacturer Purdue Pharma Pleads Guilty."
18. "Evidence."
19. "IPCC Sixth Assessment Report."
20. Newkirk II, "*Vanuatu Plan*."

is a simple reason why they don't: Right now, oil makes a lot of money. Take 2023 as an example. Three of the world's largest oil and gas producers—Exxon Mobil, Chevron, and Shell—reported combined profits of $85.6 billion in 2023.[21] "In 2023, we returned more cash to shareholders and produced more oil and natural gas than any year in the company's history," said Mike Wirth, Chevron's chairman and chief executive officer.[22]

Their messaging is often "climate positive." In fact, CNN reports that 60 percent of the 3,421 public communications released by the five major companies (BP, Chevron, ExxonMobil, Shell, and TotalEnergies) in 2021 contained at least one "green" claim.[23] To achieve global climate targets by 2030, the industry would need to spend approximately $400 million annually on clean energy. Currently, oil companies are spending far less than that, just 2.5 percent of their capital, collectively, on green power.[24] The means are clearly there in the oil industry, but the ends, that is, maintaining corporate profits, seem to be the determining factor driving spending and investment strategies.

These examples should not lead us to conclude that every business puts its pursuit of profits above all. Many companies recognize that the ends do not always justify the means. Yet this question can sometimes be ever-present for some. Indeed, it is worth noting that a basic purpose of law in this model is that it limits the goals of the business to lawful purposes and nothing else.

As relevant as the question of end versus means might be in business ethics, it is even more urgent in medicine, especially when it comes to testing new drugs.

Double-blind testing—meaning studies where neither the participants nor the experimenters know who is receiving a

21. Exxon Mobil reported $36 billion in profit for the year, supported by further oil and gas production. Chevron outlined profits of $21.4 billion—its second-largest profits in a decade. Shell reported adjusted earnings of $28.25 billion for the year, down significantly from 2022 but also the second largest in a decade.

22. Domonoske, "Making Oil is More Profitable."

23. Kent, "Big Oil Companies are Spending Millions to Appear 'Green.'"

24. Domonoske, "Making Oil is More Profitable."

Ends Versus Means

particular treatment—are seen as the most reliable type of study.[25] This procedure is utilized to prevent bias in research results, and double-blind studies are particularly useful for preventing bias due to the placebo effect. However, such studies raise a myriad of ethical issues and much has been written on ethics of such testing. Some patients in the trial receive placebos, and their illness thus remains untreated and unabated. Even those who receive the treatment being tested might in the end find that their conditions remain unchanged (because the treatment or drug is ineffective). Some testing involves healthy individuals taking the drug to better ascertain its effects on humans.

There is agreement within the medical and research communities that it is unethical to conduct double blind placebo-controlled trials where standard therapies exist, except under limited circumstances. The Declaration of Helsinki speaks directly to this issue. The World Medical Association had adopted a resolution on human experimentation in 1954. In 1964, after several revisions, the World Medical Assembly (WMA) adopted the document now known as the Declaration of Helsinki, which recommended a worldwide minimal standard for human subject research. This affirmed the WMA's position that extreme care must be taken in making use of a placebo-controlled trial. The Declaration explicitly stated that, in general, this methodology should only be used in the absence of existing proven therapy.[26]

At its core, double-blind testing comes down to means versus end. Think about it. A certain percentage of participants may become ill or may die, but what if the drug or experimental procedure is a success? How many more lives might be saved? Is this not what the ends justifying the means is all about?

While some might argue that there may be a degree of nuance when applying the concept of the ends justifying the means in the realms of business or medical ethics, most would agree that religion tends to view things in a much more "black and white" manner. Let's take the perspective of one academic, Octavio Javier

25. Ryding, "What is a Double-Blind Trial?"
26. "Declaration of Helsinki."

Esqueda, a professor at Talbot School of Theology at Biola University, as an example. Professor Esqueda concedes that justifying one's actions to achieve what he or she consider a greater good can be a very attractive temptation. However, he maintains that any action that would run contrary to the New Testament harms the reputation of Christianity. That is, the ends may not always justify the means. For Esqueda, there are no contradiction or double messages in Christian doctrine. Indeed, as he states, a Christianity that presents a contradiction between its motivations and actions does not represent Jesus.[27]

Judaism's view of means versus ends may at first glance seem equally cut and dry, but it is in fact both complex and nuanced.

It seems axiomatic that, in terms of ritual observance, Judaism rejects the idea that the ends always justify the means. Let's take a simple example to demonstrate this point. Let's say that there is a Jew who is too impoverished to purchase something needed for ritual purposes on the Sabbath (such as wine) or one of the holidays (such as matzah for Passover). His only option is to steal, either the item itself or the money to then buy the item. If he or she does any of this, the item in question is disqualified from use in any ritual purpose.[28] The Sages even went so far as to rule that blessing God with stolen goods is actually an act of cursing Him.[29] Simply put, in matters of ritual, violating a negative command (the "means") negates any "mitzvah" one might perform with the stolen item (the "ends").

For a ritually observant person, missing an opportunity to fulfill a mitzvah may be troubling, but it is neither tragic nor earth-shattering. More fundamentally, the Sages were consistent in their view that even the best of motivations (the means) never justifies bad or sinful outcomes. However, what if the question of means versus ends potentially involves the loss of life? Do we reconsider or even flip the equation? Consider the following case from the

---

27. Esqueda, "Ends Never Justifies the Means."
28. Talmud Bavli Sukkah 30a.
29. Talmud Bavli Bava Kamma 94a.

Ends Versus Means

Jerusalem Talmud, where the question at hand is this: May the few be sacrificed to save the many?[30]

The discussion centers on the incident concerning Sheba ben Bichri recorded in chapter twenty of II Samuel.[31] After Absalom's revolt against David is crushed, Sheba ben Bichri sounded a shofar and exclaimed: "We have no portion in David, No share in Jesse's son! Every man to his tent, O Israel!" In response, the men of Israel marched ahead after Sheba ben Bichri to their homeland instead of escorting David to Jerusalem.

Sheba ben Bichri's rebellious actions did not go unnoticed. Joab, commander of King David's army, pursued him, with the intent of executing him. When Joab arrived at Abel of Beth-maacah (where Sheba ben Bichri had taken refuge), Joab laid siege to the city and demanded that Sheba ben Bichri be handed over to him. Failure to comply with that demand, he threatened, would result in annihilation of all inhabitants of the city. The issue of means versus ends here is far more complex than the questions surrounding a stolen ritual item.

What to do? May the townspeople actively assist and be complicit in the death of an individual?

The Jerusalem Talmud tackles this very question and declares that a demand addressed to a community to select one or more of its members for execution must be rejected despite an accompanying credible threat to annihilate the entire community. If, however, a specific person is identified for surrender, the issue is much less clear. Indeed, the question of whether to comply with that demand is the subject of controversy among the Talmudic Sages. One maintains that compliance with the demand for the delivery of a specified individual is warranted since a greater number would perish otherwise. The opposing view disagrees and argues that the demand may be honored only if the person so identified is guilty of a capital offense as was Sheba ben Bichri.

---

30. Terumot 8:4.

31. The analysis that follows is drawn from Bleich, "Survey Of Recent Halakhic Literature, Rescue Dilemmas."

In the case of Sheba ben Bichri, both Sages would agree that he should be turned over to Joab. Nonetheless, the Talmud's initial ruling is perplexing. Why should a group of persons already marked for death (as were the inhabitants of Abel) be forbidden to deliver one of their own to the adversary who has singled out a member of the group and demanded his surrender (whether he is guilty or not)?

Part of the answer lies in the famous Talmudic dictate: "What makes you think that your blood is redder than the blood of your fellow?"[32] As one prominent contemporary rabbi writes:

> The declared postulate is that all blood is equally red. All lives are equal in value. All lives are of infinite value. The sum of many infinities is infinity. As Rashi comments, there is certainly no reason to commit an act of homicide to preserve one life over another. Consequently, one cannot claim that a single life may be sacrificed in order to preserve many lives.[33]

Then there is the Sinaitic tradition, which asserts that the severity of the prohibition against homicide prohibits the delivering an individual to an adversary even in situations where the concept of "whose blood is redder" does not apply.[34] Perhaps in the secular world, the "means" of turning over one individual to achieve the very important "ends" of saving everyone else can be justified. It is this easy within the realm of Jewish law.[35]

Another scenario with connotations of condemning people to death involves the allocation of life-saving medications and therapies during the time of medical crises. This is not a theoretical question but was the reality in parts of the United States and

---

32. Talmud Bavli Pesachim 25b.
33. Bleich, "Survey of Recent Halakhic Literature: Rescue Dilemmas," 118.
34. *Kesef Mishneh, Hilkhot Yesodei ha-Torah* 5:5.
35. While the case of Sheba ben Bichri may not be completely analogous to the ongoing hostage situation in Gaza (as we write, fifty-nine individuals who were kidnapped from Israel on October 7, 2023, remain in captivity), it does resonate deeply with us.

around the world during the coronavirus pandemic. Let us consider this issue using the rubric of means versus end.

The coronavirus pandemic was not the first time that doctors, civic leaders, and even theologians wrestled with this issue, although it had been many years. In recent years, advances in medicine and medical technology have led to the preservation of countless human lives. Yet modern medicine forced societies to confront moral quandaries that were virtually unknown in the recent past. Among them were how to allocate machinery, medicine, and medical services when they are not sufficient to save every life that might be saved. The dilemma was dramatized decades ago with the establishment of so-called God committees to assign use of the then newly invented dialysis machine to otherwise end-stage renal patients. Less dramatic, but equally vexing, are regularly made decisions regarding assignment of I.C.U. beds.[36] The coronavirus pandemic simply elevated such conundrums to new levels.

In any medical emergency, the ends are obvious. Save as many people as possible. However, in circumstances such as the recent pandemic, the means were often unclear and limited. Which patients should be put on one of the few available ventilators? If they do not respond and their condition continues to deteriorate, may they be removed from the ventilator so that a less critical patient may benefit from it and survive? What about the medications that were shown to be effective in increasing a patient's likelihood to survive but were available in limited quantities, such as remdesivir?[37] Who should get such medications? The most ill? Those most likely to survive? Young people and children? Or perhaps key personnel (such as doctors and first responders) and critical community leaders?[38]

36. Bleich, "Survey of Recent Halakhic Literature: Coronavirus Queries," 83.

37. Remdesivir, sold under the brand name Veklury, is a broad-spectrum antiviral medication developed by the biopharmaceutical company Gilead Sciences.

38. In October 2020, President Donald J. Trump was diagnosed with Covid-19 and was much sicker than publicly acknowledged at the time, with extremely depressed blood oxygen levels at one point and a lung problem associated with pneumonia caused by the coronavirus. As president, he received

In such circumstances, there was little debate about the ends (saving lives), but deciding how to deploy the means is incredibly complicated when a decision may save one life at the cost of another. Even when it is clear that the second person, even with medical intervention, will without doubt die in the foreseeable future.

Jewish law is unapologetic in its embrace of the principle of "whose blood is redder." Still, there are times that require careful consideration and weighing all the facts and all possible outcomes, and at such times, some lives are indeed saved at the cost of others.[39] Said differently, the ends might justify the means in certain emergency situations, but it is not the proper way to build a system of law, religious or secular. If we can say such a thing, God hates these emergencies, even if He does, so to speak, permit these bad outcomes in the face of impossible or unavoidable circumstances.

---

a level of medical intervention unavailable at that time to most Americans. President Trump recovered. Would citizen Trump have recovered is an interesting question.

39. In his article on the allocation of medical resources previously cited, Rabbi Bleich cites the following to illustrate how difficult it can be to weigh means and ends when lives are at risk: "The sole medical officer in an Israeli army unit was confronted with an even graver dilemma. The doctor performed emergency surgery to extract a bullet from a soldier's chest. The patient remained in serious condition requiring ventilator support and continuous monitoring while being evacuated by helicopter for hospital treatment. Battle was still raging and hence the physician's dilemma: A medic was available to accompany and monitor the patient. However, in the physician's judgment, the soldier's chances of survival would be greater if he, himself, were to accompany the patient. His problem was that in battle "The sword consumes these and those" (II Samuel 11:25), i.e., in time of war casualties must be anticipated both by the vanquished and the victor. Thus, the physician cogently feared that there would be further casualties requiring his life-saving medical attention on the battlefield. Rabbi Yitzchak Zilberstein, *Ve-Ha'arev Na*, III, 343–45, reports that his father-in-law, R. Joseph Shalom Eliashiv, ruled that the doctor should remain in the field because of the strong likelihood that there will be additional casualties. Rabbi Eliashiv's primary consideration is reported to have been that, when troops are under fire, the situation is tantamount to a *holeh le-faneinu*. An additional consideration advanced by Rabbi Eliashiv focuses upon the morale of the troops. Knowing that, should one of them be wounded, there would be no physician available to treat him, contended Rabbi Eliashiv, would create a state of fear that itself should be recognized as enhancing the danger—and that danger was certainly a present, rather than a future, danger."

Ends Versus Means

Halakha acknowledges these but steadfastly refuses to build a system of law around them.

Where then does this leave us?

It seems that the Talmudic sages intuitively grasped that the ends can almost never justify the means in day-to-day life, which would explain why, as we have previously noted, they went so far as to rule that blessing God with stolen goods is actually an act of cursing Him. Nonetheless, it is worth pausing a moment to reflect upon this rabbinic mindset before we examine the various biblical verses the Sages garner to support it. The Talmudic rabbis understood that problems on a national level differ considerably from those on a personal level, especially when weighing "means" and "ends."

The classic "Trolley Problem" will provide us with some context.

The Trolley Problem usually involves thought experiments in any number of fields, such as ethics, psychology, or artificial intelligence, that wrestle with stylized ethical dilemmas of whether to sacrifice one person to save a larger number.[40] These series often begin with a scenario where a runaway trolley or train is on course to collide with and kill a number of people (traditionally five) down the track, but a driver or bystander can intervene and divert the vehicle to kill just one person on a different track.

The Talmudic rabbis may have used different terminology, but it was clear to them that, on a personal level, sometimes Jewish ethics looks at better outcomes and permits that to be a factor in determining what choices to make. For the individual, or even for several individuals, Trolley Problem numbers do matter when deciding what to do. While the individual is never given *carte blanche* to sin, people may let sin happen when it produces good. If we think about that runaway trolley, the individual may divert it to save many lives even at the expense of others.

This, we believe, is not only eminently logical but is also grounded in a number of biblical verses, such as that found in Deuteronomy, where the Jewish people are commanded to "Do

---

40. Its origins can be traced back to a 1967 analysis of debates on abortion and the doctrine of double effect by the English philosopher Philippa Foot.

what is right and good in the sight of the LORD."[41] Or the verses in Psalms, in which David pleads with God to "let me know Your paths, O LORD; teach me Your ways; guide me in Your true way and teach me."[42]

Underlying the debate of ends versus means seems to be the notion that the means are secondary to the ends. This is why some argue that the ends, if important and desirable, always trump the means. The book of Numbers serves as a counter argument to this approach. As we will discuss in the next chapter, Moses concludes during the Jews' forty-year sojourn in the wilderness that the people need a different model of leadership. Moses as king served them well in the wilderness. Joshua as king upon their conquest of Canaan would not. Changing the leadership model is Moses's end game, his desired outcome, and what we see from his actions and decisions in Numbers is that the process of achieving this outcome is just as important, if not more important, than the outcome itself.

The question of whether the ends (i.e., outcomes) ought to drive and inform the means (i.e., processes) assumes that the latter are subordinate to the former. Moses teaches us that this is not true, and as we will ultimately show, America's founders grasped this lesson in creating a new nation and crafting a system of governance for it.

---

41. Deuteronomy 6:18.
42. Psalms 25:4–5.

Chapter Three

Moses's Backstory

WHILE THE TORAH LAYS out the foundations and the early history of the Jewish people, it provides us with surprisingly few details about the lives of the major characters in this narrative. Students of the Bible are familiar with the struggles of Abraham and Sarah to have a child and the drama surrounding Abraham's decision to offer his beloved son Isaac as a sacrifice to the Lord. They know of Jacob's encounters with Esau and with Laban and the challenges he faced in his personal life, having married two sisters, Rachel and Leah. The Patriarchs and Matriarchs lived impossibly long lives by our standards, but most of their experiences are shrouded in mystery.

This is certainly even more true for Moses. Yes, most of us have heard of Moses being placed in a basket by his mother soon after his birth only to be rescued and raised by Pharaoh's daughter.[1] Yet, the text tells us nothing of his upbringing. Was he truly part of the royal family or merely tolerated as an outsider that the Princess, for reasons beyond their comprehension, adored? Was he really a rival for the throne of Egypt as depicted in cinematic treatments

---

1. At this point in the narrative, the text does not identify by name the parents of Moses. They are simply described as "a certain member of the house of Levi" and "a woman of Levi." Exodus 2:1.

of this story?[2] We do not know the answer to such questions, but the Midrash, a compendium of the Jewish Oral Tradition, fleshes out this part of the story for us.[3] It first describes the relationship between Pharaoh's daughter and the baby Moses:

> Pharaoh's daughter used to kiss and hug Moses, loved him as if he were her own son, and would not allow him out of the royal palace. Because he was so handsome, everyone was eager to see him, and whoever saw him could not turn his eyes away from him.[4]

Midrash goes on to suggest that Moses was destined for royalty and that this would pose a danger to Pharaoh, something that we all know came to pass. Per this approach, it was only Divine intervention that prevented Pharaoh from eliminating the threat Moses represented:

> Pharaoh also used to kiss and hug him, and Moses used to grab Pharaoh's crown and put it on his own head. The magicians of Egypt sitting there said, "We fear this one who grabs your crown and puts it on his own head may be the one, as we have been saying, who will take your kingdom away from you." Some of the magicians suggested that he be slain, others that he be burned alive. But Jethro, who sat among them, said, "This child has yet no understanding. Why not test him? Place before him a vessel with a gold piece and a burning coal in it. If he reaches for the gold, he has understanding, and you may slay him. But if he reaches for the coal, he has no understanding, and a sentence of death is not called for." The items were brought at once. Then, as Moses put forth his hand to grab the gold, Gabriel came down and shoved it to the side, so that

---

2. As seen in films such as *The Ten Commandments* (1956) and *The Prince of Egypt* (1998).

3. Midrash falls into two categories. When the subject is law and religious practice (*halakha*), it is called *midrash halakha*. The second, *midrash aggadah*, interprets biblical narrative, exploring questions of ethics or theology, or creating homilies and parables based on the text. The latter were compiled between about 200 and 1000 CE. We will rely upon these in exploring Moses's backstory. "What is Midrash."

4. Exodus R. 1:26.

Moses's Backstory

Moses not only seized the coal but also put the hand with the coal into his mouth and burned his tongue. As a result he became slow of speech and slow of tongue.[5]

The biblical text, having passed over his childhood without comment, continues the narrative of Moses's life without a specific chronological reference, simply stating that "when Moses had grown up, he went out to his kinsfolk and witnessed their labors."[6] Again, many are familiar with the rest of the story. Moses goes out to observe the plight of the Hebrew slaves. He sees an Egyptian taskmaster beating "one of his kinsmen."[7] The text tells us that Moses kills the Egyptian and hides his body in the sand, without informing us of his motivation. Yet, we need not speculate why Moses undertook such a bold and dangerous action, killing an Egyptian taskmaster to spare the life of a Hebrew slave. The Midrash spells it out for us:

> What preceded the Egyptian's beating the Hebrew? [The account that follows will explain]: The taskmasters were Egyptian, but the foremen were Israelite, one taskmaster over ten foremen, and one foreman over ten Israelites. The taskmasters used to go around early in the morning to the foremen's homes to get them out to work at cockcrow. Once an Egyptian taskmaster saw an Israelite foreman's wife, Shelomith, the daughter of Dibri, who was beautiful-free of any blemish-and he cast his eye upon her. So, the next day at cockcrow, he went to that foreman's home and quietly said to him, "Go, gather your team of ten men." Then he hid himself behind the staircase. The moment the husband left, the Egyptian got into the bed chamber and defiled the woman. It so happened that the husband turned back and saw the Egyptian as he was leaving the house. The husband reentered his house and asked his wife, "Did the Egyptian touch you?" She replied, "Yes, but I thought it was you!"

---

5. Exodus R. 1:26.
6. Exodus 2:11.
7. Exodus 2:11.

> When the taskmaster became aware that the husband had found him out, he put the husband back to heavy labor and beat him all day, saying, "Work harder, work harder," trying to kill him. Through the holy spirit, Moses saw what the Egyptian had done to the Hebrew in his home and what he intended to do to him in the field and said: "It is not enough for this wicked one that he defiled the wife-he is also determined to kill the husband."[8]

Here, the Midrash provides us with important insights into Moses's character, his abhorrence of injustice and his great concerns for others. Even as a prince of Egypt, he sees the deep injustice in his adopted society. These traits will guide him when he ultimately confronts Pharaoh and during his forty years of leadership of the Jewish people in the wilderness.

Pharaoh learns of Moses's actions and seeks to kill Moses. He flees to Midian. There, he takes a wife after saving her and her sisters from hostile shepherds while the women were out tending to their father's flocks. How long was Moses in Midian? What did he do there? How did his stay in Midian prepare him for the task of leading the Hebrews out of slavery? The biblical text provides no answers. However, the Midrash gives a marvelous account of Moses's life after fleeing Egypt.[9] In brief, Moses was eighteen when he fled Egypt. He ultimately arrived in Cush, which is ancient Ethiopia, where he waged war on behalf of King Kokinus who had been deceitfully ousted by the wicked Balaam (a former advisor to Pharaoh), who also bewitched the people and cunningly fortified the city. After nine years of fighting, Moses successfully re-conquered the capital. By this time, the former and rightful king dies, and the grateful populace declares Moses their new king. They even gave him the widowed Queen Adoniya as his wife.[10]

Moses's reign lasts for forty years (until the age of sixty-seven), until the disgruntled idolatrous queen beseeches the populace

---

8. Exodus R. 1:28–29.

9. Yalkut Shimoni, 1:168; Sefer HaYashar, Parashat Shemot.

10. According to the Midrash, Moses never consummates the marriage because of the Queen's idolatrous ways.

Moses's Backstory

to dethrone Moses in favor of Munchan, her son from Kokinus. Due to their great love for Moses, they are reluctant to do so, but Moses cedes the crown voluntarily. The people then send him off with great honor and gratitude. At this point, Moses finally travels to Midian where he resides with Yitro for ten years before marrying Yitro's daughter Tzipora at the age of seventy-seven.[11]

Military leader. Tactician. King. These very much describe the Moses of the Exodus story and of the Jews' forty years in the wilderness. We once again see here how the Midrash aligns Moses's backstory with the narrative given to us in the biblical text.

There yet remains the question of why Moses? Did his life experiences make him uniquely qualified to lead the Jewish people? Perhaps, but the Midrash goes on to offer two additional reasons for God choosing Moses to lead the Hebrews out of Egypt.

The first addresses Moses as a shepherd for the sheep of his father-in-law Jethro. It once happened that one of the sheep ran away. Moses ran after it until it reached a small, shaded place. There, the lamb came across a pool and began to drink. According to the Midrash, as Moses approached the lamb, he said, "I did not know you ran away because you were thirsty. You are so exhausted!"[12] He then put the lamb on his shoulders and carried him back. The Holy One said, "Since you tend the sheep of human beings with such overwhelming love—by your life, I swear you shall be the shepherd of My sheep, Israel." This tale is meant to inform us of Moses's deep commitment to the individual, not just to the community, one of the virtues that would come to characterize him as a leader.[13]

The second focuses on Moses's encounter with the burning bush, a miraculous sight he beheld while searching for his lost sheep. The verse describes Moses's first reaction thusly: "I must

---

11. This midrashic timeline runs counter to the simple reading of the text in Exodus. This is to be expected, as midrash is not meant to convey the simple reading of the verse. Rather, it is intended to share a grander moral vision of the text.

12. Exodus R. 2:2.

13. Exodus 3:3.

turn aside to look at this marvelous sight."[14] The assumption in the rabbinic literature is that other passersby had seen this burning bush, but only Moses "turned aside" to investigate. Only he was prompted to draw near to discover why the bush burned but was not consumed, an act that highlighted his daring and intellectual curiosity.

In sum, the real purpose of the many midrashic tales that seek to fill in Moses's "backstory" is to provide us with a deeper vision of Moses's upbringing. What we see time and time again in those texts is an individual practicing being a good leader and thus building a skill set he will need for later in his life.

While these last two stories give us a fuller understanding of how and why Moses comes to his leadership position, the text itself makes clear, Moses did not aspire to this: "Who am I that I should go to Pharaoh and free the Israelites from Egypt?"[15] Moses served because he was needed. This allowed him to easily accept his changing roles throughout the forty years in the wilderness as recorded in the book of Numbers. He identified what was needed and stepped up to do it. In doing so, be it knowingly or unwittingly, he created a leadership model that he could pass down to future generations of Jewish leaders.

---

14. Exodus 3:3.

15. Exodus 3:11. The Midrash, as quoted by the medieval commentary Baal HaTurim on Leviticus 9:1 ("On the eighth day Moses called Aaron and his sons, and the elders of Israel."), quotes Moses as saying: "because I refused [to lead the Jewish people] for seven days at the burning bush, I only merited to serve [as Kohen Gadol] seven days."

Chapter Four

Moses's Leadership Roles Prior to Korah's Rebellion

As we just noted, Moses may have been a reluctant leader, but he was both skilled and experienced. Hence, it is not surprising that the people accepted him as their leader upon his return to Egypt from Midian:

> Then Moses and Aaron went and assembled all the elders of the Israelites. Aaron repeated all the words that the LORD had spoken to Moses, and he performed the signs in the sight of those assembled, and the assembly was convinced. When they heard that the LORD had taken note of the Israelites and that [God] had seen their plight, they bowed low in homage.[1]

This is how we tend to think of Moses, as the leader who confronts Pharaoh and leads the people out of Egypt. While true, we would argue that Moses at this point is more like God's "frontman." Moses of course is the greatest prophet of the ancient Israelites.[2] He

---

1. Exodus 4:29–31.
2. "Never again did there arise in Israel a prophet like Moses—whom Hashem singled out, face to face" (Deuteronomy 34:10).

communicated the very words God spoke to both the Pharaoh and the Hebrew slaves. Nonetheless, the text clearly states that it was God Himself who freed the Jews from bondage "by a mighty hand, by an outstretched arm and awesome power, and by signs and portents."[3] To this day, Jews around the world acknowledge and expound upon this at their Seder tables when reciting this verse from the Passover Haggadah and then commenting: "not by an angel and not by a seraph and not by a messenger, but rather the Holy One of Blessing Himself." Moses is at some level merely an agent of God in the Exodus story. Indeed, when Jews gather yearly to commemorate the Exodus at the Passover seder, Moses is unmentioned—as if we would tell the story of American independence without mentioning George Washington!

This is not to diminish the role Moses plays in the Exodus from Egypt. Rather, we highlight this so as to begin our discussion of Moses's changing leadership roles as he evolved post-Exodus, since Exodus is arguably the "Godliest" period in the Torah.

To be clear, we are not the first or only authors to write about the changing leadership roles of Moses. Among our favorites is the very fine work written by Rabbi Mosheh Lichtenstein.[4] Another outstanding scholar, Dr. Stephen Garfinkel, sums up the matter quite concisely: "In most cases, Moses' skills were consistent with the needs of the community even as those needs shifted, and his ability to summon different talents at different times may have been one of Moses' most valuable leadership assets. . . . Moses needed to apply different skills in different circumstances, and he generally managed to do so quite masterfully."[5]

Unlike these other works, our focus is not on the hows or whys that underlie the various leadership mantles Moses assumes throughout the biblical narrative. We are instead interested in what America in the twenty-first century can learn from the model of governance Moses sought to instill in the Jewish people.

---

3. Deuteronomy 26:8.
4. Lichtenstein, *Moses*.
5. Garfinkel, "The Man Moses, the Leader Moses," 21–22.

Moses's Leadership Roles Prior to Korah's Rebellion

Said differently, this book is not about the Bible, but rather about what the Bible can teach Americans.

Without question, as the Jews enter the Sinai wilderness, Moses continues to be God's prophet, just as he was in Egypt, but now he is also something like a king whose authority is not to be questioned. He is the law giver, and, at first, he alone adjudicates legal disputes, sitting "as magistrate among the people, while the people stood about Moses from morning until evening."[6] His father-in-law Jethro witnesses this and questions the wisdom of this approach: "What is this thing that you are doing to the people? Why do you act alone, while all the people stand about you from morning until evening? . . . The thing you are doing is not right."[7]

We often think of ancient kings as despots who brooked no questions about or challenges to their authority. Perhaps the most infamous example was the Roman emperor Caligula, who ruled from 37 CE until his assassination in 41 CE. The few surviving sources about his four-year reign portray Caligula as a self-indulgent, cruel, sadistic, extravagant, and sexually perverted insane tyrant who demanded and received worship as a living god, humiliated his Senate, and planned to make his horse a consul. And who has not heard of France's King Louis XIV's statement to the Parliament of Paris in 1655, "L'État, c'est moi" ("I am the state")?

How then did Moses react to Jethro's criticism? He listened carefully to Jethro's subsequent suggestion to "seek out, from among all the people, capable individuals who fear God—trustworthy ones who spurn ill-gotten gain" and then to "set these over them as chiefs of thousands, hundreds, fifties, and tens, and let them judge the people at all times."[8] Jethro was urging Moses to give up, voluntarily, some of his absolute authority, and Moses did so. Here we see the first sign that Moses understood an absolute monarchy would not be in the Jewish people's best long-term interest. It also marks the beginning of Moses elevating and emphasizing the means (i.e., the judicial process and the creation of law)

6. Exodus 18:13.
7. Exodus 18:14, 17.
8. Exodus 18:21–22.

instead of simply focusing on the ends (i.e., the judicial outcome). One cannot appoint judges without eventually creating law. This idea—that courts create law—is a central tenet that produces the common law and the American legal system. Judges need law to adjudicate, otherwise there would just be arbitrary outcomes.

It is important to note that Moses's absolute power in civil matters extended to ritual matters, as well. It was he who ascended Mount Sinai to speak to God "face to face" and received His law on behalf of the people. It was also Moses who performed the sacrificial rites when the Tabernacle was first erected. According to the Midrash, Moses only performed these duties for seven days as a consequence of his arguing with God before agreeing to be the leader of the Jewish people. On the eighth day after the inauguration of the Tabernacle, Moses's brother Aaron assumes the role of High Priest (*Kohen Gadol*), and his sons take on the role of Priests. Moses had no choice but to accede to God's directive, but he did so with no complaints. This, too, suggests that Moses was inclined to pursue a decentralization of power. How so? Law and courts diminishes the authority of the ruler. Thus, the grandest contribution Moses makes is that law binds him and is above the leadership. The centrality of law—above the leadership and binding on the leadership—is the central contribution of the Jewish tradition to law.

This trend becomes much more pronounced in the book of Numbers. Indeed, it is the theme of the book, one which ultimately envisions processes (means) taking precedence over outcomes (ends). This is all about how law ought to work—law ought not be a dictatorship by judges, but an adjudicative system that works to fairly and consistently resolve disputes so that similar disputes are resolved similarly. This idea is extremely important. Law is about the fair application of consistent principles. This is what the Bible is saying to America here.

The narrative itself in Numbers is rather complicated. The consensus in the rabbinic literature is that there has never been a generation as great as the one that left Egypt, neither before nor since. They alone merited a national encounter with the Divine at

Moses's Leadership Roles Prior to Korah's Rebellion

Mount Sinai,[9] and yet, God declares that this generation tested Him repeatedly in the Sinai wilderness (Numbers 14:22). When exactly did the people test God? The Talmudic sages provide us with the details:

> Our ancestors tested the Holy Blessed One ten different times. These are the ten: Once at the sea, once when the manna was first given, once when the manna stopped coming down, once at the first appearance of quails, once at the latter appearance of quails, once at Marah, once at Refidim, once at Horev, once [at the Calf, and once] with the spies.[10]

Over the centuries, biblical commentators have offered many explanations for each of these episodes. While their approaches may differ, they all echo (to various degrees) a common theme in Judaism, namely, that the greater the individual, the more closely and even harshly are his or her actions judged by God.[11] The best example of this is Moses himself.

Towards the end of the Jews' travels through the wilderness, at a place called Meribah, Moses hits the rock to bring forth water for the thirsty people instead of speaking to it as God commanded. Why Moses ignores God's explicit command is too complicated to delve into here, but in the end, God acquiesces. Water gushes from the rock, which is a great miracle whether the rock was struck or spoken to. Nonetheless, God tells Moses: "Because you did not trust Me enough to affirm My sanctity in the sight of the Israelite people, therefore you shall not lead this congregation into the land that I have given them."[12] One misdeed, and a seemingly minor one at that, and Moses is denied his life-long dream: to lead the people into the Holy Land.

---

9. This stands in stark contrast to the other monotheistic religions Christianity and Islam. Only their founders had direct encounters with the Divine.

10. Avot DeRabbi Natan 9:2. Avot DeRabbi Natan is the first and longest of the minor tractates of the Talmud.

11. Talmud Bavli Sukkah 52a.

12. Numbers 20:12.

The notion that "righteous leadership" is often judged more harshly helps explain the "angry" God that is so prominent in the book of Numbers. This, however, is not germane to our analysis of Moses's changing leadership role. What is more important is how Moses reacts to each of these ten tests and what his reactions tell us about his leadership style at that particular moment.

There is one additional element to these tests, and this, too, is related to the dimensions of Moses's leadership. The stories in Numbers often reflect God's desire that the Jewish people grow into a self-governing nation. To achieve this, God must step back, as it were. The spiritual bond between God and the people remains strong. In Egypt, God declares that "Israel is My first-born son," and despite the rebellious and at times sinful nature of the people in the wilderness, God's fidelity to His people and the covenant He made with them remains constant.[13] Nonetheless, God's visible intervention in their lives decreases, which aids in Moses's efforts to teach the people about the need to lead themselves.

Let us now explore those episodes which most demonstrate this. While we will examine each in the order in which they appear in Numbers, there are two narratives worth considering independently as they will help frame our discussions of the evolving interactions between God, Moses, and the Jewish people.

The first is the biblical commandment to wear a fringed garment:

> Speak to the Israelite people and instruct them to make for themselves fringes on the corners of their garments throughout the ages; let them attach a cord of blue to the fringe at each corner.[14] That shall be your fringe; look

---

13. Exodus 4:22.

14. A close reading of this verse makes clear that there are two requirements: One is to affix white fringes on the corners of a four-cornered garment, and the other is to add a thread of *tekhelet* (described in the rabbinic literature as "sky blue") to each corner. These two requirements are independent of each other. When *tekhelet* is available, a *tekhelet* fringe must be added to the *tzitzit*; when unavailable, one can fulfill the commandment with plain white fringes. For generations, the unique dye used to make this shade of blue was made from a byproduct of a sea creature known as the *chilazon*, which lives in the

Moses's Leadership Roles Prior to Korah's Rebellion

at it and recall all the commandments of Hashem and observe them, so that you do not follow your heart and eyes in your lustful urge. Thus you shall be reminded to observe all My commandments and to be holy to your God. I Hashem am your God, who brought you out of the land of Egypt to be your God: I, your God Hashem.[15]

To be clear, this commandment does not refer only to the prayer shawls (*tallit*) traditionally worn by men (and some women in non-Orthodox denominations). Rather, it is a self-standing commandment to attach fringes (*tzitzit*) to any four-cornered garment.

In biblical times, men often wore such garments, which to a modern observer would appear akin to a poncho with some sort of belt around the middle. However, those garments differed in one significant way from our ponchos. In the ancient Near East, as portrayed in art and literature, we see that these garments had a hem, and not just any hem. Hems were "an extension of its owner's person and authority." Indeed, the more important the individual, the more elaborate the embroidery of his hem."[16] The Bible itself reflects this when it tells us that David cut off the hem of Saul's garment but later felt remorse for doing so. Saul, in reflecting on the significance of this act, observed: "Now I know that you [David] will indeed reign."[17]

Mediterranean Sea. At a certain point in history, approximately 1,000 years ago, the *chilazon*, which was always hard to come by—to the extent that the Talmud (Menachot 44a) notes that it surfaced only once every seventy years—became unavailable altogether. Ultimately, its exact identity became unknown, and subsequently, *tzitzit* worn by Jews only had white threads. In modern times, the marine snail *Murex trunculus* has been identified as possibly being the elusive *chilazon*, and today many use its dye to add a blue thread to their *tzitzit*. "Tekhelet."

15. Numbers 15:38-41.
16. Jacob Milgrom, quoted in Lockshin, "What Do Tzitzit Represent?"
17. 1 Samuel 24:3-21.

Illustration of David Cutting off a Piece of King Saul's Robe while he slept in a cave (Samuel). Painting by Henry Coller. Image courtesy of ALAMY.

What was the reason for David's remorse and Saul's response? The answer rests in the meaning of the hem: it was an extension of Saul's person and authority. David felt remorse for taking it because God had not so ordered. Saul, however, regarded it as a sign from God that his authority had been transferred to David: he was now cut off from the throne.[18]

For the Jews of antiquity, *tzitzit* were a way of extending the hem. The significance of such an elaborate hem "lies in this: it was

---

18. Jacob Milgrom, quoted in Lockshin, "What Do Tzitzit Represent?"

worn by those who counted: it was the ID of nobility."[19] How so? Seeing the *tzitzit* was intended to remind the wearer that he, as a Jew, was a member of God's "kingdom of priests." (Exodus 19:6) The Talmudic sages, as only they can, put a fine point on the extent to which *tzitzit* serve as a reminder:

> There was an incident involving a certain man who was diligent about the mitzva of ritual fringes. This man heard that there was a prostitute in one of the cities overseas who took four hundred gold coins as her payment. He sent her four hundred gold coins and fixed a time to meet with her. When his time came, he came and sat at the entrance to her house. The maidservant of that prostitute entered and said to her: That man who sent you four hundred gold coins came and sat at the entrance. She said: Let him enter. He entered. She arranged seven beds for him, six of silver and one of gold. Between each and every one of them there was a ladder made of silver, and the top bed was the one that was made of gold. She went up and sat naked on the top bed, and he too went up in order to sit naked facing her. In the meantime, his four ritual fringes came and slapped him on his face. He dropped down and sat himself on the ground, and she also dropped down and sat on the ground. She said to him: I take an oath by the gappa of Rome that I will not allow you to go until you tell me what defect you saw in me. He said to her: I take an oath by the Temple service that I never saw a woman as beautiful as you. But there is one mitzva that the Lord, our God, commanded us, and its name is ritual fringes, and in the passage where it is commanded, it is written twice: "I am the Lord your God" (Numbers 15:41). The doubling of this phrase indicates: I am the one who will punish those who transgress My mitzvot, and I am the one who will reward those who fulfill them. Now, said the man, the four sets of ritual fringes appeared to me as if they were four witnesses who will testify against me.[20]

---

19. Jacob Milgrom, quoted in Lockshin, "What Do Tzitzit Represent?"
20. Talmud Bavli Menachot 44a.

Yet, let us not forget the reciprocal nature of the *tzitzit*. Not only does it remind the wearer of his Jewish identity and all that entails, as the verse says, "thus you shall be reminded to observe all My commandments." The *tzitzit* also alerts other members of the community of the wearer's strong ties to the community. It is as if the wearer is declaring, behold, I am a member of this historic group of people called Jews.[21] Building community is an important goal so long as community reenforces law obedience.

There is a final aspect to *tzitzit* that touches upon Moses's desire to help the Jewish people evolve into a self-governing nation. As modern Biblical scholar Jacob Milgrom writes: "The *tzitzit* are the epitome of the democratic thrust within Judaism, which equalizes not by leveling but by elevating. All of Israel is enjoined to become a nation of priests ... *tzitzit* is not restricted to Israel's leaders, be they kings, rabbis or scholars. It is the uniform of all Israel."[22]

A final point. *Tzitzit* were so much a part of a Jew's self-identification with his faith and his people that when four-cornered garments became passée, Jews were unwilling to give up this mark of distinction. They accepted upon themselves the custom of wearing a small, four-cornered garment (properly called *tallit katan*, or small *tallit*, but more commonly referred to simply as *tzitzit*).[23] They of course did so in order to fulfill the biblical commandment, but in doing so, they were also continuing to express their

---

21. This is how the wearing of *tzitzit* was described in a moving article by Eugen Schoenfeld, who described himself at the age of ninety as "not a died-in-the-wool Orthodox Jew [but rather] at best ... a historical Jew with a traditional heart." See "One Man's Opinion–The Tallit."

22. Milgrom, *Numbers*, 414.

23. The prevailing custom per rabbinic decree was to wear this small garment as part of one's daytime attire. Since it had a fixed time frame, women were exempted from this rabbinic ordinance per the Talmudic ruling that "with regard to all positive, time-bound mitzvot, i.e., those which must be performed at specific times, men are obligated to perform them and women are exempt (Kiddushin 29a). This does not mean that women are prohibited from wearing *tzitzit*. They are not, and some do. However, this is rare in contemporary Orthodox communities. For more on this topic, see Lockshin, "What Do Tzitzit Represent?"

connection to the Jewish people.[24] Wearing *tzitzit* in our times thus represents both the fulfillment of a biblical obligation and a sign of national self-identification. It also reflects obedience to law which is also part of community.

With most countries, the idea of national self-identification is linked to its system of governance. Part of an American's national identity is defined by the country's standing as one of the world's oldest democracies. One's British identity, as just another example, often reflects one's ties to the monarchy.[25] In biblical Israel, this was also true, although in the many centuries of exile following the destruction of the Second Temple and the Jew's banishment from their homeland by the Romans in 68 CE, outward manifestations of Jewish identity such as *tzitzit* took on new-found importance.

A second narrative that provides a backdrop to our main thesis involves the perplexing biblical commandment of the *Sotah* (Numbers 5:11–31). *Sotah* is the term used by the Torah to describe a woman who has been accused by her husband of marital infidelity even though there are no witnesses to support his allegations. Without witnesses, the husband cannot press his claims in

---

24. Throughout the ages, there have been different practices regarding keeping the actual *tzitzit* fringes tucked into one's pants or out. Some, like the Chassidim, wear their *tzitzit* garment over their shirts, while others, most often Jews of European descent (Ashkenazim), wear them under their shirts. Then there are Jews from Spain and the Middle East (Sephardim), who generally do not keep their *tzitzit* out, although many nevertheless do so. For a fuller discussion of this topic, see Lebovits, "Tzitzis In Or Out?" and Enkin, "Tzitzis In or Out?"

25. In the last poll conducted in her lifetime, 81 percent of people in Great Britain had a positive opinion of Queen Elizabeth II (See "Share of Respondents in Great Britain Advising"), a figure that reenforces the notion that the British national identity is linked to one's ties to the monarchy. This, however, may be somewhat less true today given the many kerfuffles committed by the Royal Family since Elizabeth's passing. Indeed, her successor, King Charles III, only ranks fourth among the royals in popularity, with 56 percent holding a favorable view and 21 percent unfavorable. (The Prince and Princess of Wales are the most popular members of the Royal Family, each with 69 percent reporting a favorable view of them.) Skinner, Public Perceptions of the Royal Family Improve as Prince and Princess of Wales Remain the Most Popular and Over Half Believe King Charles is Doing a Good Job."

a *beit din* (a Jewish court of law). Nonetheless, the Torah permits him to bring his wife before a priest in the Temple in Jerusalem, who in turn takes some earth from the floor of the Temple and adds it to some sacral water in an earthen vessel. What follows is the only trial by ordeal found in Jewish law:

> The priest shall adjure the woman, saying to her, "If no other party has lain with you, if you have not gone astray in defilement while living in your husband's household, be immune to harm from this water of bitterness that induces the spell. But if you have gone astray while living in your husband's household and have defiled yourself, if any party other than your husband has had carnal relations with you"—here the priest shall administer the curse of adjuration to the woman, as the priest goes on to say to the woman—"may Hashem make you a curse and an imprecation among your people, as Hashem causes your thigh to sag and your belly to distend; may this water that induces the spell enter your body, causing the belly to distend and the thigh to sag." And the woman shall say, "Amen, amen!"[26]

After this oath is administered, the priest writes these curses on a scroll using ink that is dissoluble in water. He then pours some of the water and earth concoction over the scroll, and the woman is made to drink the rest. At this point the ordeal begins:

> Once he has made her drink the water—if she has defiled herself by breaking faith with her husband, the spell-inducing water shall enter into her to bring on bitterness, so that her belly shall distend, and her thigh shall sag; and the wife shall become a curse among her people. But if the woman has not defiled herself and is pure, she shall be unharmed and able to retain seed.[27]

How are we to understand such an anomaly in Jewish law? No witnesses. No judges. No testimony. Instead, we have nothing more than these "water of bitterness," but the water itself is harmless.

26. Numbers 5:19–22.
27. Numbers 5:27–28.

Moses's Leadership Roles Prior to Korah's Rebellion

We dare not forget that it is God who punishes or rewards. If she is innocent, the falsely accused woman is absolved. If guilty, God afflicts her with their physical effects: miscarriage, infertility, or even death.

Some have described the *Sotah* ritual as "magical and horrifying."[28] Yet, the fact is there is little evidence that this ritual ever took place. In the Torah itself, the law is given without a connection to any particular incident. Moreover, the Mishnah tells us that Rabbi Yochanan ben Zakkai nullified the ritual entirely.[29] Not because of any actions on the part of Jewish women. Rather, says the Mishnah, Rabbi Yochanan took this dramatic step because the number of men committing adultery had increased significantly. How could the rabbinic leadership seek to punish women merely suspected (without proof no less!) of adultery when the husbands themselves were guilty of this sin? It is thus unsurprising that the entire body of rabbinic literature cites only one example of its implementation.[30]

Notwithstanding this uncertainty regarding the reality of the *Sotah* ritual, its narrative leaves many modern readers unnerved. This is understandable, as this biblical ritual sounds uncomfortably like trial by ordeal, evoking specters of barbaric medieval justice such as burning the accused's hand with hot iron or dunking the accused in cold water to determine guilt or innocence.[31] This discomfort is further reflected in modern scholarship, which often focuses on the gender inequality inherent to the ritual, and it is hard not to see gender inequality in the traditional rabbinic literature.

The Mishnah and Talmud detail a humiliating procedure in which the woman is brought to the Temple, frightened with stories of biblical adulterers, then debased by having her hair uncovered, jewelry removed, and some of her clothing torn.[32] This procedure

---

28. Berkun, "Redeeming the Sotah."
29. Talmud Bavli Sotah 9:9.
30. Grushcow, "Sotah: Understanding Change."
31. Lindell, "Was the Sotah Meant to be Innocent?"
32. Mishnah Sotah 1:4–6; Sotah 7b.

seems designed to produce a confession before she had to drink,[33] a point Maimonides emphasized in his legal code.[34] If she is guilty, according to the Mishnah, it seems as though she dies a gruesome death.[35] Tellingly, the Mishnah says nothing about the possibility of her innocence. In the rabbinic view, even if the waters found her innocent, she still bears some measure of guilt, as she inappropriately secluded herself with another man after being warned not to do so.[36] After all this, innocence almost seems a side point: the rite was administered in a way that all but assumes the woman's guilt.[37]

In response to all this, three Jewish interpreters from different religious backgrounds proposed an alternative reading of the narrative. Rather than seeing the *Sotah* ritual as ordeal at all in the traditional sense, each of the three—R. Herbert Chanan Brichto, an academic Bible scholar and dean of the Reform Hebrew Union College, R. Emanuel Rackman, a Modern Orthodox thinker at Yeshiva University who later became president of Bar Ilan University in Israel, and R. Yaakov Kamenetsky, student of the famed Slobodka Yeshiva in Europe and Rosh Yeshiva of Torah Vodaath in Brooklyn—independently argued that the point of the *Sotah* ritual was to find the woman innocent and to allow her to return to her marriage.[38]

Crucial to understand this is the recognition that the *Sotah* ritual needed a miracle to punish the accused woman, not a miracle to acquit her. This stands in sharp contrast to the Salem witch trials, where a miracle was needed to exonerate the witch.

How does this new understanding of the *Sotah* relate to our thesis? We will demonstrate in the coming pages that Numbers portrays time and time again God's desire for the Jewish people to become a self-governing nation. To achieve this, God must step back, and the *Sotah* ritual, at least as understood by Rabbis Brichto,

33. Mishnah Sotah 1:5.
34. Mishneh Torah Hilkhot Sotah 3:2–3.
35. Mishnah Sotah 1:7, 3:5.
36. Mishnah Sotah 1:1—1:2.
37. Lindell, "Was the Sotah Meant to be Innocent?"
38. Lindell, "Was the Sotah Meant to be Innocent?"

Rackman, and Kamenetsky, illustrates this. God seeking justice and doing justice goes to the core of Jewish beliefs. What greater justice is there than allowing a falsely accused woman prove her innocence? Here, however, with the *Sotah*, God opts not to act independently. Granted, the ritual itself is seemingly at odds with more normative Jewish law, but it allows for human involvement, by the woman who must voluntarily drink the bitter waters and by the priest who facilitates the ritual. Yet the idea that God should regularly come down from heaven and do divine justice in this world was not a model of Jewish national life that was sustainable.

This approach to the *Sotah* is supported by modern scholarship on medieval trials by ordeal. This idea that such ordeals were meant for the innocent, not the guilty, seems rather obvious upon careful reflection. Since people believed in the ordeal's efficacy, the guilty would confess in order to avoid injury. Only the innocent would put themselves to the test. The priests, knowing this, would rig medieval ordeals so that they tended to vindicate the accused, such as by lowering the temperature of the boiling water so that the burn would heal faster and be interpreted as a sign of innocence from God.[39]

The priest in the Temple certainly could not nor would not "rig" the ordeal. However, by bringing the matter to this priest, an emissary of God, it is clear to all, including and especially the husband, that God's justice, not flawed human justice, has prevailed.[40]

With our thesis contextualized, we now move on to the specific narratives in Numbers.

"IF ONLY WE HAD MEAT TO EAT!"

The first story we will consider is set forth in chapter eleven. The narrative heard opens with a troubling phrase: "The people took to complaining bitterly before Hashem."[41] The text gives us no reason

---

39. Lindell, "Was the Sotah Meant to be Innocent?"
40. Lindell, "Was the Sotah Meant to be Innocent?"
41. Numbers 11:1.

for their bitter complaints, but the medieval commentators are quick to provide one. One approach suggests that the complaints were unfounded and that the people were seeking a pretext to distance themselves from God.[42] Another view posits that the people were simply feeling sorry for themselves given the circumstances they faced in the wilderness.[43]

As the text makes clear, God was not pleased with their complaints. If the people merely sought to provoke God, they were successful. To the extent that their complaints were an outgrowth of self-pity, God found this unacceptable, as they should have followed Him "in joy and gladness over the abundance of everything."[44] Regardless of the cause, God's reaction was swift and fierce: "Hashem heard and was incensed: a fire of Hashem. broke out against them, ravaging the outskirts of the camp."[45] Only due to Moses's intervention (he prayed to God) does the fire die down, and the people are saved. But the story and the people's complaints do not end here:

> The riffraff in their midst felt a gluttonous craving; and then the Israelites wept and said, "If only we had meat to eat! We remember the fish that we used to eat free in Egypt, the cucumbers, the melons, the leeks, the onions, and the garlic. Now our gullets are shriveled. There is nothing at all! Nothing but this manna to look to!"[46]

The seeming disgust the people felt towards the manna is incomprehensible, at least in the midrashic literature. The Torah itself describes the manna in sparse terms: "Now the manna was like coriander seed, and in color it was like bdellium."[47] In compari-

---

42. See Rashi on Numbers 11:1. He further points out that the Hebrew for "people" (*am*) always denotes wicked men.

43. See Nachmanides on Numbers 11:1.

44. Deuteronomy 28:47

45. Numbers 11:1.

46. Numbers 11:4–6.

47. Numbers 117. Bdellium is a fragrant resin produced by several trees related to myrrh, used in perfumes.

son, the Midrash waxes eloquently about the miraculous nature of the manna:

> Manna is described in Scripture as "bread, as "honey," and as "oil." How are the differing descriptions to be reconciled? Young men tasted in it the taste of bread; old people the taste of honey; and infants the taste of oil.[48]

> "And the taste of it was the taste of a cake (*leshad*) baked with oil" (Numbers 11:8) R. Abbahu said: Read not *leshad*, "cake," but *shad*, "breast." Hence, just as an infant, whenever he touches the breast, finds many flavors in it, so it was with manna. Whenever Israel ate it, they found many flavors in it.[49]

Given the manna's flavorful and diverse taste, why would the people crave meat? The manna could have had beef-like flavor for those who wished for this. And why the nostalgic (and starkly false) reminiscences about their diet in Egypt? Their servitude was incredibly harsh, and their diet, quite meager!

Consistent with His reaction to the people's previous unprovoked complaints. God is none too pleased. His first reaction, to use modern parlance, is rather "snarky":

> And say to the people: Purify yourselves for tomorrow and you shall eat meat, for you have kept whining before Hashem and saying, "If only we had meat to eat! Indeed, we were better off in Egypt!" Hashem will give you meat and you shall eat. You shall eat not one day, not two, not even five days or ten or twenty, but a whole month, until it comes out of your nostrils and becomes loathsome to you. For you have rejected Hashem who is among you, by whining before [God] and saying, "Oh, why did we ever leave Egypt!"[50]

---

48. Exod. R. 25:3.
49. Talmud Bavli Yoma 75a.
50. Numbers 11:18–20.

The real punishment, the real display of God's anger and involvement in the lives of the people, only comes once the people begin their "feasting" on the promised meat:

> A wind from Hashem started up, swept quail from the sea and strewed them over the camp, about a day's journey on this side and about a day's journey on that side, all around the camp, and some two cubits deep on the ground. The people set to gathering quail all that day and night and all the next day—even the one who gathered least had ten *chomers*—and they spread them out all around the camp. *The meat was still between their teeth, not yet chewed, when the anger of Hashem blazed forth against the people and Hashem struck the people with a very severe plague.*[51]

And what of Moses? When the people complained, and God smote them with fire, the people's first reaction was to "cry out" to Moses. Moses hears their pleas, prays to God, and the fire immediately abated.[52] Yet here, in the face of the people's demands for meat, Moses seems overwhelmed. The man who stood up to Pharaoh and brought fearsome plagues upon Egypt, the man who assuaged the people's fear of imminent destruction at the shore of the Sea of Reeds[53] by exclaiming: "Have no fear! Stand by, and witness the deliverance which Hashem will work for you today,"[54] cries out in despair to God:

> And Moses said to Hashem, "Why have You dealt ill with Your servant, and why have I not enjoyed Your favor, that You have laid the burden of all this people upon me? Did I produce all these people, did I engender them, that You should say to me, 'Carry them in your bosom

---

51. Numbers 11:31–33. Emphasis added.
52. See Rashi on Numbers 11:2.
53. The Torah describes Moses splitting the *yam suf*. The same phrase appears in over twenty other places in the Hebrew Bible. It has traditionally been interpreted as referring to the "Red Sea," following the Greek Septuagint's rendering of the phrase. However, the correct translation of the phrase is "Sea of Reeds," although its exact location is unknown.
54. Exodus 14:13.

as a caregiver carries an infant,' to the land that You have promised on oath to their fathers? Where am I to get meat to give to all this people, when they whine before me and say, 'Give us meat to eat!' I cannot carry all this people by myself, for it is too much for me. If You would deal thus with me, kill me rather, I beg You, and let me see no more of my wretchedness!"[55]

This, we believe, is a significant turning point in Moses's approach to leading the Jewish people. As Rabbi Joseph B. Soloveitchik[56] describes it:

> These are words which were never uttered by Moshe. It is true that he uttered a similar phrase when he was sent to Pharaoh on his first errand and his mission ended with complete failure. He came back to God and said: Hashem, why have you mistreated this people? Why did you ever send me? This was the question of a young, inexperienced man. But Moshe, the leader who took the people out of Egypt, never repeated the question. It is not Moshe-like to act like a frightened person and to speak out of the depths of resignation and to condemn the people.[57]

According to Rabbi Soloveitchik, up to this point, Moses was convinced that he and the Jewish people were in the midst of the final journey to the Promised Land. (It is important to remember that this incident occurs prior to the people's sin with the golden calf.) No delays, no procrastination, no if, and no when—but as soon as possible. "Suddenly, something happened. Neither Moses nor anybody else expected the event to transpire. What happened? ... [T]he multitude that was among them felt a lust, had a

---

55. Numbers 11:11–15.

56. Rabbi Joseph B. Soloveitchik was a renowned Talmudist, halakhic authority, and theologian and one of the most creative and influential Jewish thinkers of the twentieth century. Known to his followers as The Rav (literally, "the rabbi"), he ordained thousands of Orthodox rabbis over the course of his career, and his students and philosophy continue to impact the Jewish world today. Goodman, "Joseph Soloveitchik."

57. Rabbi Yitzchak Etshalom, "Rav Soloveitchik's Lecture on Leadership."

desire. And *B'nei Yisrael* [the Jewish people] wept again and they said: Who shall give us flesh to eat?"[58]

In response, Moses feels great resentment. He was deeply angry, so much so that it was evil in his eyes, and thus, he could not, would not offer prayers on behalf of the people.[59] He sees the people working all that day and night and all the next day, too, gathering the quails. The least anyone gathered was ten *chomer* (roughly 57.5 gallons![60]), and afterwards, they spread the quails out for themselves all around the camp. Witnessing this, Moses realizes that perhaps this generation, the one that endured years and years of harsh enslavement, did not have what it takes to enter and then conquer the Promised Land. He understands for the first time that, to achieve God's goal for the Jewish people, they will need a different model of governance. They should not depend on a Moses, one who is Oracle and Lawgiver and Teacher and Judge, one is akin to a king and even beyond. This people need to become more independent. They need to learn how to govern themselves, and this prompts Moses's plea to God: "I cannot carry all this people by myself, for it is too much for me." God agrees and tells Moses:

> Then [God] Hashem said to Moses, "Gather for Me seventy of Israel's elders of whom you have experience as elders and officers of the people and bring them to the Tent of Meeting and let them take their place there with you. I will come down and speak with you there, and I will draw upon the spirit that is on you and put it upon them; they shall share the burden of the people with you, and you shall not bear it alone.[61]

Here it starts, the process of the decentralization of civil power and authority. Moses has begun to step back from miraculous leadership. God on the other hand? Not yet. That will come later in Numbers.

58. Etshalom, "Rav Soloveitchik's Lecture on Leadership."
59. "Moses heard the people weeping, every clan apart, at the entrance of each tent. HASHEM was very angry, and Moses was distressed," Numbers 11:10.
60. "Chomer."
61. Numbers 11:16–17.

Moses's Leadership Roles Prior to Korah's Rebellion

"MIRIAM AND AARON SPOKE AGAINST MOSES BECAUSE OF THE CUSHITE WOMAN"

Before we turn to the narrative set forth in chapter twelve of Numbers where Moses's siblings discuss his personal life, it is worth reflecting on the relevance of Moses's personal life to his evolving leadership style.

Americans may not condone their presidents for having extramarital affairs, but they have certainly become accustomed to this reality. Historical records show that Franklin D. Roosevelt had a long-running romantic affair with Lucy Mercer Rutherfurd, who ultimately became his wife's social secretary. While the affair predated his presidency, there is some evidence Roosevelt's affair with Rutherfurd likely continued into his presidency.[62] John F. Kennedy's affairs were numerous and legendary. Lyndon B. Johnson is said to have had multiple affairs that his wife ignored. Barbara Bush's biographer wrote that she was suicidal over George H. W. Bush's affair that reportedly lasted eighteen years.[63] Aside from Bill Clinton's multiple affair allegations, he was also accused of sexual assault. Lastly, Donald Trump has an extensive history of misconduct allegations and rumored affairs.

Many in secular societies compartmentalize such misconduct. People tend to think that these affairs have little or no effect on a president's style of governance or his policy decisions. And this, for the most part, may be true.[64] However, this is not the case in religiously based governance, and it is not merely due to issues of immortality. Let us explain.

The question of the celibacy of the priestly class has historically been linked to one's position in the world. How so? Vows of celibacy by the clergy were seen as evidence of an individual's devotion to a higher calling. More significantly, celibacy was

---

62. Details of this affair as well as the others mentioned in our text are cited in Balevic, "9 US Presidents Who Faced."

63. Page, *Matriarch*.

64. One glaring exception is the impact Clinton's sexual dalliances with Monica Lewinsky and his subsequent impeachment had on his second term in office. See for example Sarver, *Effects of the Impeachment on Bill Clinton's Staff*.

considered a vehicle for setting apart the clergy from the masses through their rejection of the physical for the spiritual.

The best-known example of this is the Catholic Church, although this has not always been the case. Peter, the first pope, and the apostles that Jesus chose were, for the most part, married men. Married men were leaders of the Church until the fourth century, but in 306 CE, the Council of Elvira, Spain, decreed that a priest who sleeps with his wife the night before Mass will lose his job. The Council of Nicea, held in 325 CE, went even further and decreed that a priest could not marry after ordination.

These decrees were not universally accepted, however, as historical records show. For instance, Siricius only left his wife to become pope in 385 CE.[65] In 567 CE., the Second Council of Tours ruled that any cleric found in bed with his wife would be excommunicated for a year and reduced to the lay state. French documents from the seventh century show that most priests were married. In the eighth century, St. Boniface reported to the pope that in Germany almost no bishop or priest was celibate. In the ninth century, the Council of Aix-la-Chapelle (836 CE) openly admitted that abortions and infanticide took place in convents and monasteries to cover up activities of uncelibate clerics.[66] It is only in 1074 CE, when Pope Gregory VII decrees that men who wish to be ordained must first pledge celibacy, that the matter is finally settled as Church doctrine.[67]

Fueling this centuries-long push for celibacy among Catholic clergy are a few key passages in the New Testament. Take Matthew 19:12, where he clearly commends those who are celibate "for the sake of the kingdom of God." Paul is even more explicit:

---

65. As pope, he did not require that priests not be married, but he ultimately declared that married priests may no longer sleep with their wives. "Brief History Celibacy in the Roman Church."

66. "Brief History Celibacy in the Roman Church."

67. Settled as official policy but not necessarily accepted, as some historians maintain that as late of the fifteenth century, 50 percent of priests were married and accepted by the people. "A Brief History Celibacy in the Roman Church."

Moses's Leadership Roles Prior to Korah's Rebellion

> I wish that all were as I myself am. But each has his own gift from God, one of one kind and one of another. To the unmarried and the widows I say that it is good for them to remain single, as I am. But if they cannot exercise self-control, they should marry. For it is better to marry than to burn with passion.[68]

Paul reiterates and expands upon this in 1 Corinthians:

> I would like you to be free from concern. An unmarried man is concerned about the Lord's affairs—how he can please the Lord. But a married man is concerned about the affairs of this world—how he can please his wife—and his interests are divided. An unmarried woman or virgin is concerned about the Lord's affairs: Her aim is to be devoted to the Lord in both body and spirit. But a married woman is concerned about the affairs of this world—how she can please her husband. I am saying this for your own good, not to restrict you, but that you may live in a right way in undivided devotion to the Lord.[69]

What is the practical implications for the Church of a celibate clergy? As the *Catholic Encyclopedia* makes clear, Catholic clergy are above and apart from those they serve:

> The laity and clergy, or clerics, belong to the same society, but do not occupy the same rank. The laity are the members of this society who remain where they were placed by baptism, while the clergy, even if only tonsured, have been raised by ordination to a higher class, and placed in the sacred hierarchy.[70]

In contrast, Judaism neither endorses nor embraces any notion of life-long celibacy.[71] Indeed, the very first commandment set forth in the Pentateuch, given to Adam and Eve and then again to Noah when he and his family emerge from the ark, is to be "fruitful

---

68. 1 Corinthians 7:7-9 NIV.
69. 1 Corinthians 7:32-35.
70. "Laity." Emphasis added.
71. Of course, Judaism only sanctions sexual intimacy in the context of marriage, something the Catholic Church tried for centuries to ban among its clergy.

and multiply."[72] The biblical Patriarchs and Matriarchs are sorely pained by their difficulties in having children. When God appears to Abraham and tells him that his reward will be very great, Abraham responds: "O lord, Hashem, what can You give me, seeing that I shall die childless, and the one in charge of my household is Dammesek Eliezer!"[73] Isaac and Rebekah pray regularly and intensely for twenty years so as to be blessed with children.[74] When Rachel sees that her sister and co-wife Leah has borne four sons to Jacob, she exclaims: "Give me children, or I shall die."[75]

The Talmudic Sages also extol the virtues of marriage and children. Their take on the topic was perhaps best summarized by Ben Sira, when he stated: "A good wife is a good gift for her husband. And it is written: A good one will be placed in the bosom of a God-fearing man; a bad wife is a plague to her husband."[76] The Talmudic Sages as well as all the great rabbis of subsequent generations were married, some more happily than others. Among their numbers there was but one notable exception, Simeon ben Azzai, or as he is more commonly referred to, Ben Azzai. Ben Azzai never married, and it is worthwhile considering how the Talmudic text addresses his decision.

> It is taught in a *baraita* that Rabbi Eliezer says: Anyone who does not engage in the mitzva to be fruitful and multiply is considered as though he sheds blood, as it is stated: "Whoever sheds the blood of man, by man shall his blood be shed" (Genesis 9:6), and it is written immediately afterward: "And you, be fruitful and multiply" (Genesis 9:7). Rabbi Ya'akov says: It is as though he diminishes the Divine Image, as it is stated: "For in the image of God He made man" (Genesis 9:6), and it is written immediately afterward: "And you, be fruitful and multiply" (Genesis 9:7). Ben Azzai says: It is as though he sheds blood and also diminishes the Divine Image, as it is stated: "And you, be

72. Genesis 1:28, 9:1.
73. Genesis 15:2.
74. Genesis 25:21.
75. Genesis 30:1.
76. Talmud Bavli Yevamot 63b.

fruitful and multiply," after the verse that alludes to both shedding blood and the Divine Image. They said to ben Azzai: There is a type of scholar who expounds well and fulfills his own teachings well, and another who fulfills well and does not expound well. But you, who have never married, expound well on the importance of procreation, and yet you do not fulfill well your own teachings. Ben Azzai said to them: What shall I do, as my soul yearns for Torah, and I do not wish to deal with anything else. It is possible for the world to be maintained by others, who are engaged in the mitzva to be fruitful and multiply.[77]

How can one so praise the virtues of sexual intimacy and rearing children and still refrain from both? To use the Catholic idiom, Ben Azzai saw himself as married to God, or at the very least, married to His Torah.

Frankly, the Sages were perplexed by Ben Azzai's life choices. While they never condemned him and even recognized his lifestyle as an option, they discouraged others from following Ben Azzai's example. In the end, other than the occasional rare individual such as Ben Azzai, celibacy was never followed in practice in the Jewish world.

What follows from this is very important. Jewish religious leaders and teachers were married. They were sexually active. In this regard, they saw themselves as similar to the masses. These religious leaders in no way thought that sexual relations with their spouses distanced them from God. Indeed, the reverse is true. They understood that sex is not merely something driven by lust or intended solely to produce children. They believed that sexual intimacy between a husband and wife can and ought to be elevated and sanctified. And when practiced in this manner, it fulfills the Divine mandate that a man should leave his father and mother and cling to his wife, "so that they become one flesh."[78]

What can and should we glean from this? Simply put, we see that a sexually active clergy is no closer nor more distanced from God than the masses. One's relationship with God in Judaism is

77. Talmud Bavli Yevamot 63b.
78. Genesis 2:24.

about following God's commandments, studying His laws, and doing acts of righteousness and kindness. Everyone is capable of doing each of these based on his or her abilities and level of commitment. This accords with the well-known Mishnaic teaching: "There are three crowns: the crown of Torah, the crown of priesthood, and the crown of royalty, but the crown of a good name supersedes them all."[79] In other words, even those not blessed with superior intellect or born into the priesthood or royalty can achieve greatness. Hence, there is no religious hierarchy in Judaism. To the contrary, when it comes to spiritual and religious leaders, Judaism is very much a meritocracy, as demonstrated by the number of converts to Judaism who, over the centuries, became some of Judaism's greatest and most important teachers.[80]

With this as context, we can better parse the discussion between Miriam and Aaron about their brother Moses's personal life. In doing so, we will see that this is much more than just another story about siblings bickering amongst themselves.

At first glance, the genesis of this discussion seems clear: "Miriam and Aaron spoke against Moses because of the Cushite woman [*isha kushit*] he had taken [into his household as his wife]: "He took a Cushite woman!"[81] However, this verse is shrouded in ambiguity. It is well-known that Moses's wife, Zipporah, is from Midian, not Cush, which is traditionally thought to be an ancient territory located near the Red Sea[82] as seen in

---

79. Pirkei Avot 4:13.

80. Among the greatest Sages whose teachings were disseminated in the Talmud and who were also converts were Shemaya and Avtalyon, who are included in the list of generational leaders in Pirkei Avot; Rabbi Meir, whose influence was so great that any anonymous Mishna set forth in the Talmud is credited to him; and Rabbi Akiva, who is described (Talmud Bavli Menachot 29b) as follows: When Moshe ascended to the heavens, he found the Holy One, Blessed be He, sitting and attaching crowns to the letters. He said before Him, "Master of the Universe! Who is staying your hand?" He said to him, "There is one man who will exist after many generations, and Akiva the son of Yosef is his name, who will in the future expound on every crown and crown piles and piles of laws."

81. Numbers 12:1.

82. "The Kingdoms of Kush." Modern translations of the Bible often use the terms Ethiopia and Ethiopian as translations for Kush and Kushite

the maps below.[83] Who, then, is this Cushite woman, and why are Miriam and Aaron troubled by Moses's marriage to her? There are several approaches in the rabbinic literature that seek to answer these questions.

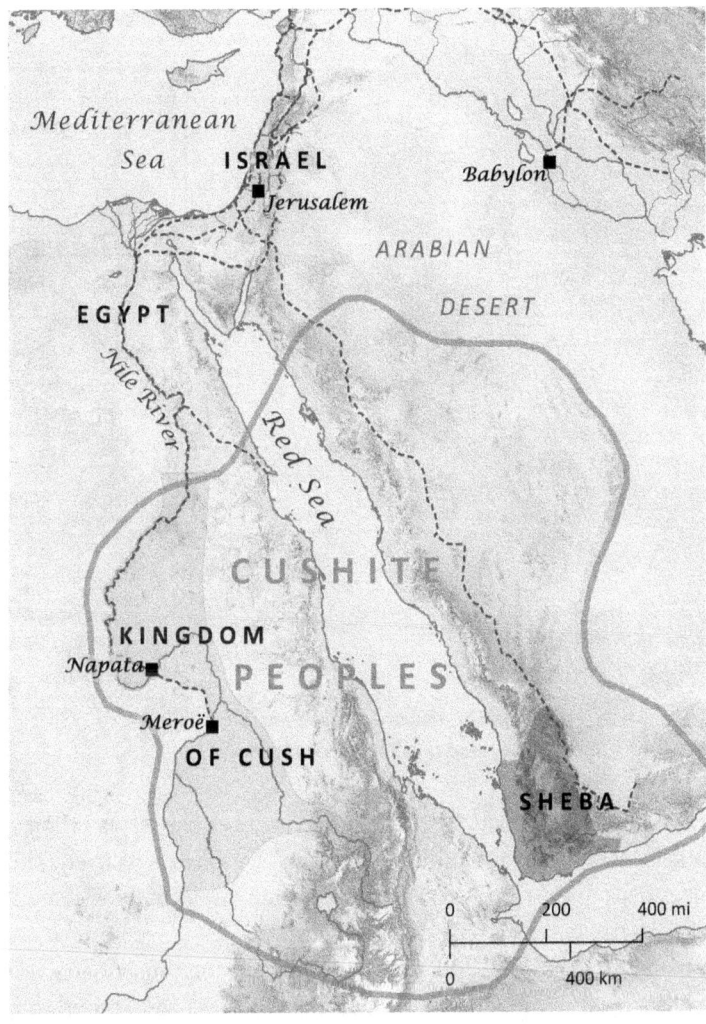

respectively. This goes back to the early Greek and Latin translations of the Hebrew. Goldenberg, "Moses' Kushite Wife Was Zipporah the Midianite."

83. Map of Kingdon of Cush courtesy of Kubek15—Own work, CC BY-SA 4.0. Map of biblical Midian courtesy of Bible Atlas.

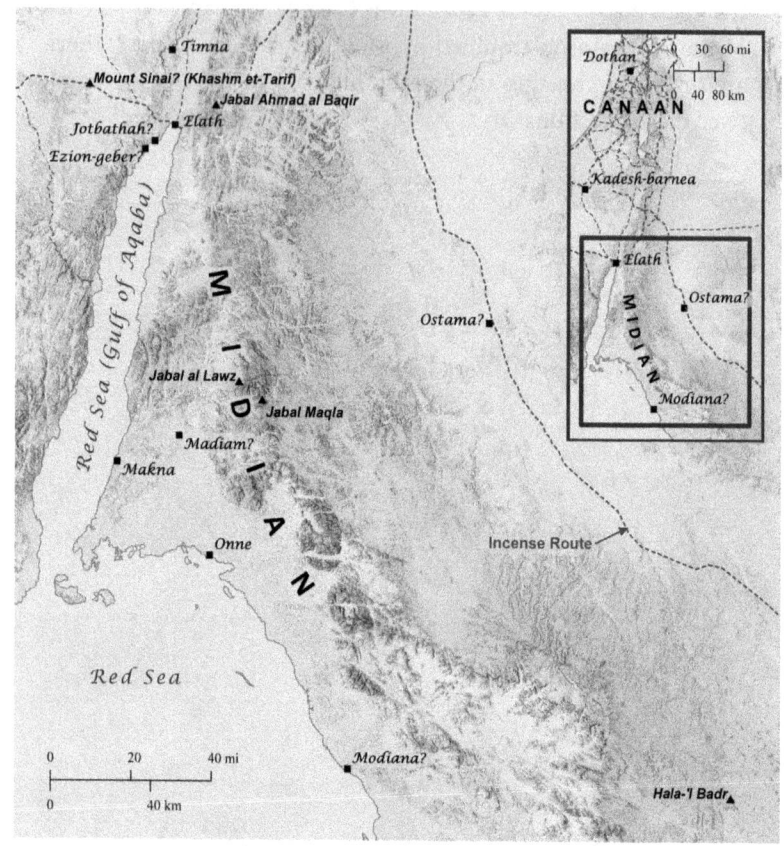

Kush and Midian are on opposite sides of what is today called the Gulf of Suez!

Modern translations of the Bible often use the terms Ethiopia and Ethiopian as translations for Cush and Cushite respectively. This goes back to the early Greek and Latin translations of the Hebrew.[84] If our verse is indeed referring to African Cush, it reflects one of two possibilities: either a different tradition about the country of origin of Moses's wife Zipporah or the belief that Moses had a second wife, someone other than Zipporah. Some among the medieval biblical

---

84. In the Greek- and Latin-speaking world of antiquity, "Ethiopia" meant Black Africa. Goldenberg, "Moses' Kushite Wife Was Zipporah the Midianite."

Moses's Leadership Roles Prior to Korah's Rebellion

commentators[85] take the verse at its simple meaning, namely, that Moses had a second wife, from Nubia. Their reading of the verse is supported by midrashim[86] as well as by the first century Jewish historian, Flavius Josephus.[87] Collectively, these sources relate that Moses traveled to Cush before arriving many years later in Midian. In Cush, Moses is said to have married a queen. Moses becomes a great general and leads her armies to victory. He may even and ultimately have become the king of Cush.[88] This narrative not only

85. Rashbam, Chizkuni and R. Joseph Bekhor Shor.
86. *Divrei HaYamim shel Mosheh*, *Sefer HaYashar*, and *Yalkut Shimoni*.
87. Schneider, "Moses in Cush: Development of the Legend."
88. *Yalkut Shimoni* details the story thusly: War was waging between Cush and Bnei Kedem. Kukanus, King of Cush, went to war with Aram and Bnai Kedem, and he left Balaam and his sons to guard the city . . . Balaam advised the people remaining in the city to rebel against the King . . . When the King returned he saw that Balaam and his sons had made the city impregnable . . . At the time of this siege, Moses had run away from Egypt {to Ethiopia} and met the soldiers of King Kukanus who were unable to enter their city. The King and all the officers and soldiers were enamored with Moses because he looked as strong as a lion and his face shone like the sun, and they made him an advisor to them. After nine years [remaining on the outskirts of the city] the King became ill and died . . . The officers and soldiers asked Moses to lead them. And he was made King and was to be given the Lady Cushite, the wife of the late King Kukanus, as his wife. Moses was 27 years old when he became King of Cush. . .and sat upon the throne, put on the crown and took the lady Cushite as his wife. But Moses was fearful of the God of his forefathers, and he did not consummate the marriage with the lady Cushite. Moses remembered the oath that Abraham made his servant Eliezer take when he told him not to take a wife for his son from the daughters of Canaan. And Isaac did the same thing when Jacob ran away from Esau, and he told him not to marry from the children of Ham. . .and Moses was afraid from his God and acted in truth with all his heart and did not stray from the path that Abraham, Isaac and Jacob followed. And Moses ruled the people of Cush for forty years. And he was successful because the God of his fathers was with him. In the fortieth year of his reign, one day he was sitting on the throne next to Lady Cushite, and she mentioned the following to the Ministers and to the Nation: 'Forty years this King is ruling Cush, and he has not been intimate with me, and has never worshipped our Cush gods.' She asked the Ministers to appoint her son Munhas to be King, rather than the foreigner Moses. And that's what happened. Moses was 67 years old when he left Cush. He couldn't return to Egypt, from where he had run away. He ran off to Midian, to Re'uel . . . and he received Zipporah the Midianite as his wife.

enhances the reputation of Moses prior to his becoming the leader of the Jewish people but also explains that the Cushite woman was a different wife and not Zipporah.

Circling back to our discussion of clerical celibacy, this approach to the identity of the Cushite woman is wholly consistent with the Jewish tradition that religious leaders ought to marry. Why, then, are Miriam and Aaron so aggrieved by this? We know that Moses was married to his wife Zipporah for more than forty years. Presumably he loved her, but even if he did not, can there be any reason other than a desire for a sexual relationship in marrying a beautiful Cushite woman so much younger than him? Are Miriam and Aaron embarrassed by Moses's behavior? Do they find his behavior at odds with his role as spiritual leader of the Jewish people? Or perhaps are they simply envious of his physical vigor and sexuality even at an advanced age?

In this scenario, the reasons for why Miriam and Aaron question Moses's behavior is irrelevant. Their discussions border on gossip mongering, and the Pentateuch repeatedly and forcefully condemns gossiping.[89] God's harsh response, which we will examine in detail below, is both quick and understandable. Gossiping is unacceptable in general, but even more so when done by communal leaders such as Miriam and Aaron about the absolute leader of the community, Moses.

There is a second and more commonly accepted understanding of who the Cushite woman is. The traditional rabbinic interpretations of this narrative identify Zipporah as the Cushite woman with several different reasons put forward for this claim. In one approach, the term "Cushite" is understood to mean "beautiful."[90] Others see Cushite as a descriptor of her appearance, maintaining that she was either unusually dark-skinned or homely.[91] There are

---

89. The verse explicitly states: "Do not go about as a talebearer among members of your people." (Leviticus 19:16) The Talmud highlights the detrimental impact of gossiping when it says (Talmud Bavli Arakhin 15b) that gossip "kills" three people—the speaker, the recipient and the subject.

90. Sifre 99. This is the view followed in Onkelos in his Aramaic translation of the Torah.

91. Radak, R. Bechaye, Ibn Ezra, Chizkuni.

others that argue that Cushite was a type of contrary nickname,[92] one given because she was actually strikingly beautiful, and it was customary to give a superior person a less-becoming nickname, so as not to arouse jealousy.[93] Yet another explanation for Cushite is found in the Talmud. The term does not describe her appearance but rather her actions: "But is her name Cushite? Zipporah is her name. Rather, just as a Cushite is distinguished by his dark skin, so too, Zipporah was distinguished by her actions."[94]

Why do these varied sources reject the notion that Moses had a second wife? To some extent, these sources reflect the Talmudic desire to endorse monogamy.[95] More fundamentally, they all follow the general midrashic approach to biblical characters for whom little or no information is given in that they are equated to other biblical figures. They also serve to limit the number of women Moses was married to, to one who is Zipporah. Defining the Cushite women as Zipporah also better positions us to answer the second and more significant question of why Miriam and Aaron were so concerned with the details of Moses's personal life.

The most frequently given answer in the rabbinic literature is that Miriam and Aaron were discussing Moses's withdrawal from his one and only wife and his lack of physical intimacy with her, which implied to them, again in the Catholic sense, that Moses viewed himself as married to God. Like all Jewish men, Moses abstained from intercourse with his wife immediately prior to receiving the Torah at Mount Sinai. Once the Sinai experience was complete, married couples resumed intimacy, except for Moses. According to the Midrash, after the Giving of the Torah, God

92. Targum, Sifri quoted in Rashi.
93. Schneider.
94. Talmud Bavli Moed Katan 16b. We should note that many of these midrashim recount how Zipporah's beauty was preserved in her old age. This was presumably done to aggrandize Moses. He did not withdraw from his wife because she aged or because she was no longer desirable in his eyes; rather, his abstinence resulted from a divine command. Kadari, "Zipporah: Midrash and Aggadah."
95. See generally our book on Genesis, *Sex in the Garden*. We believe that the Torah limited its tales of polygamous relationships to Genesis.

instructed Moses: "Go, say to them, 'Return to your tents.' (Deuteronomy 5:26–27) But you remain here with Me"—Israel shall return to their wives, but you shall not return to marital relations.[96]

How would Miriam have known this? Modesty and decorum would seem to dictate that this remains a private matter between Moses and Zipporah. The Sages offer a few possible answers. According to one tradition, Miriam saw that Zipporah no longer adorned herself with women's jewelry, and asked her: "Why have you stopped wearing women's ornaments?" Zipporah answered: "Your brother no longer cares about this." Thus, Miriam learned that Moses had abstained from intercourse.[97]

Another exegetical tradition posits that Miriam was standing next to Zipporah when Moses was informed that "Eldad and Medad are acting the prophet in the camp!"[98] The Midrash tells us that Zipporah, upon hearing this report, said: "Woe to their wives. They will be prophets, and they will withdraw from their wives, as my husband withdrew from me." In this way, Miriam learned that Moses abstained from relations with Zipporah, and she told this to Aaron.[99]

In a third midrashic depiction, Miriam learned of Zipporah's lack of intimacy with Moses after the appointment of the seventy elders. All Israel kindled lamps and engaged in celebrations, rejoicing at the elders having attained their exalted status. When Miriam saw the lamps, she exclaimed: "Happy are these, and happy are their wives!" Zipporah corrected her: "Do not say, happy are their wives, rather, woe to their wives. From the day that God spoke to Moses your brother, he has not lain with me."[100]

It is here that this third approach differs significantly. It provides us with additional details, telling us that Miriam immediately went to Aaron and discussed the matter with him. They said: "Moses is haughty. The Lord has already spoken with many prophets,

---

96. Tanhuma, Zav 13.
97. Sifrei on Numbers ch. 99.
98. Numbers 11:27.
99. Tanhuma, Zav 13.
100. Sifrei Zuta 12:1.

Moses's Leadership Roles Prior to Korah's Rebellion

and with us as well, but we did not abstain from our spouses as Moses has done."[101] Most significantly, this final Midrash seems to best explain God's harsh reaction to Miriam and Aaron's discussion of Moses's personal life:

> Suddenly Hashem called to Moses, Aaron, and Miriam, "Come out, you three, to the Tent of Meeting." So the three of them went out. Hashem came down in a pillar of cloud, stopped at the entrance of the Tent, and called out, "Aaron and Miriam!" The two of them came forward; and [God] said, "Hear these My words: When prophets of Hashem arise among you, I make Myself known to them in a vision, I speak with them in a dream. Not so with My servant Moses;[102] he is trusted throughout My household. With him I speak mouth to mouth, plainly and not in riddles, and he beholds the likeness of Hashem. How then did you not shrink from speaking against My servant Moses!" Still incensed with them, Hashem departed. As the cloud withdrew from the Tent, there was Miriam stricken with snow-white scales! When Aaron turned toward Miriam, he saw that she was stricken with scales.[103]

Two points emerge from this alternative but logical reading of the Miriam and Aaron narrative. First, it highlights for us how unique Moses was in the pantheon of great leaders of the Jewish people. The verses here remind us that, at Sinai, Moses spoke with God face-to-face (whatever that means!). This point is reiterated in Deuteronomy where we are told that "Never again did there arise in Israel a prophet like Moses—whom Hashem singled out,

---

101. Sifrei Zuta 12:1.

102. The translation here, as it is in many other English translations, misses an importance nuance to this verse. The Hebrew actually reads: "not so with My servant, with Moses." Rashi is quick to point out the significance of the correct reading of the Hebrew verse: "It does not say 'against My servant, Moses,' but rather 'against My servant, against Moses.' This signifies 'against My servant' even if he were not as exalted as Moses, and 'against Moses' even if he were not My servant—in either case you ought to have had fear of him, and all the more so when he is My servant, and the servant of a king is like a king!"

103. Numbers 12:4–10.

face to face."[104] The greatness of Moses makes his determination to transition the people away from an absolute leader to a system of self-governance quite remarkable. Moreover, it explains why Moses's decision to abstain for sexual intimacy with his wife (per the alternative reading of this narrative) makes perfect sense in his context, but how that abstention is ultimately and definitively rejected as a norm for future Jewish religious leaders.

Second, this story is another example how, at this point in the wanderings in the wilderness, God is intensely involved with the day-to-day lives of the Jewish people. No detail is to be overlooked, not even Moses's sex life (or lack thereof). It also highlights a non-reproducible feature of the life in the wilderness: the regular, ongoing Divine intervention that could not be continued ever again. This, in turn, goes to the heart of our book, namely, that life with a regular, ongoing relationship with God is not the same as one with a distant God who gave the law and then "went away." Jewish law as we know it—and as it has existed for centuries—is built on this very notion.

"SEND AGENTS TO SCOUT THE LAND OF CANAAN"

The story we encounter in chapters thirteen and fourteen is well-known, that of Moses sending forth twelve men to scout out the land of Israel. Its ending is a calamity for the Jewish people. Yet, it seemed to be a natural and logical continuation of Moses's first steps towards decentralizing power away from himself, at least in the judicial realm, that we saw in chapter eleven.

Let us start with a point of clarification. The men Moses sends forth are commonly called "spies." Yet, the Hebrew term used at the onset of the narrative is "men" (*anashim*), not "spies" (*meraglim*). This is not a trivial linguistic matter. In the ancient world, spies, or more correctly, scouts were often employed by the military in their campaigns.[105] Indeed, not only is spying mentioned in many an-

---

104. Deuteronomy 34:10.
105. Russell, *Information Gathering in Classical Greece*, chapter three.

Moses's Leadership Roles Prior to Korah's Rebellion

cient religious texts and Homer's Iliad, but we also have evidence of spying in ancient Egypt as far back as 3500 years ago.[106] The question is thus, were the men Moses sent forth scouts in a military sense, or did he have some other purpose in mind?

The narrative here begins with a verse that has been subject to much debate in the rabbinic literature. God speaks to Moses and tells him to send forth men (not spies!), but in doing so, the verse contains what seems to be a superfluous word. God does not command, "send." Rather, He says, "send for yourself."[107] What is the intent of this phrase, for yourself? The most commonly given explanation, although not universally accepted by the medieval commentators, is that God, with this simple phrase, is empowering Moses to make the decision as to whether to send these men. This, of course, begs the question, why send them forth at all? Did God not perform wonderous miracles for the Jewish people with the plagues He inflicted upon Egypt and then at the splitting for the Sea of Reeds? Would He not do so again during the Jews' invasion and conquest of the land of Canaan? To answer these questions, we need to understand what prompted this mission and what it was intended to accomplish.

Here, in chapter thirteen, it appears that the decision is Moses's to make. Send for yourself, if you wish! However, in the book of Deuteronomy, which comprises Moses's farewell address to the Jewish people prior to his death, Moses explains to this new generation, one which did not live through foundational events such as the Exodus, the backstory of this mission:

> I said to you, "You have come to the hill country of the Amorites which our God Hashem is giving to us. See, your God Hashem has placed the land at your disposal. Go up, take possession, as Hashem, the God of your fathers, promised you. Fear not and be not dismayed." Then all of you came to me and said, "Let us send agents (*anashim*) ahead to reconnoiter the land for us and bring back word on the route we shall follow and the cities we

---

106. Thomas, "Tips for Students."
107. Numbers 13:2.

shall come to." I approved of the plan, and so I selected from among you twelve participants, one representative from each tribe.[108]

How do we reconcile these two accounts? God certainly gave Moses the option of sending men, be they spies or scouts or some other sort of other delegation. Nevertheless, is it possible that Moses only opted to use this option once the people approached him with their request?[109] Did he delay telling the people that he might in fact send forth somebody in order to give the people a say in the matter? By doing so, is he trying to impart to the people the notion that process can be as important as outcome?

We believe so. Yet regardless of the whys underlying this mission, it ended terribly. Upon their return, the men made their report public, instead of first privately sharing their findings with Moses. They began by extolling the virtues of the land ("it does indeed flow with milk and honey"), but concluded in an ominous and negative manner:

> "We cannot attack that people, for it is stronger than we." Thus they spread calumnies among the Israelites about the land they had scouted, saying, "The country that we traversed and scouted is one that devours its settlers. All the people that we saw in it are of great size; we saw the Nephilim there—the Anakites are part of the Nephilim—and we looked like grasshoppers to ourselves, and so we must have looked to them."[110]

---

108. Deuteronomy 1:20–23.

109. It is worth noting that one prominent commentator, Ovadia ben Jacob Sforno (1475–1549), understands God's use of the word *lecha* as instructing Moses NOT to allow the selection of the *anashim* to be made by the people themselves. As he writes: "We know from Deuteronomy (1:22) that the initiative of sending out spies came from the people and that Moses was put under pressure to do this. God was cautioning Moses that by allowing the people to select the spies themselves, that if they chose unsuitable candidates and they came back with a faulty report, the people would blame God for what was wrong with the country instead of the inadequate ability of the spies to correctly evaluate what they had seen."

110. Numbers 13:31–33.

Moses's Leadership Roles Prior to Korah's Rebellion

How did things go so awry? It must be that Moses and the people had very different understandings of the rationale for sending leaders to see what the situation was in the territory to be conquered. Moses understood that there was no need to send them. What did it matter what they reported back? That the inhabitants of Canaan were fierce warriors? That their cities were well fortified? God was with the Jewish people, and just as He brought them forth from Egypt and saved them at the sea, He would insure their ultimate conquest of Canaan.

What, then, did Moses hope to accomplish by sending forth these *anashim*? A close reading of the Hebrew text makes matters clear, especially when we look to the book of Joshua for some context. In preparation for the conquest of the land of Canaan, Joshua sends out spies as we tend to think about the term. These men were sent out "secretly," and their mission was "reconnoiter (*re'u*) the region of Jericho."[111] The narrative here makes it quite clear that their mission was to identify weak spots in the defenses of the walled city of Jericho. However, they were not as stealthy as they ought to have been, as the verse attests: "The king of Jericho was told, 'Some men have come here tonight, Israelites, to spy out the country.'"[112]

Now consider the mission at hand. Moses does not send them forth to spy, *leragel*, but rather *lasur et ha'aretz*, to scout the land.[113] He sent them to search and explore. Theirs was not a military intelligence, but rather a study expedition, and they were to submit a number of reports, including a demographic report ("Are the people who dwell in it strong or weak, few or many?") and an agricultural report (Is the soil rich or poor? Is it wooded or not?").

This interpretation of this mission as non-military in nature is further by the choice of the men themselves. Moses did not send professional spies or even miliary men. He instead sent political leaders ("each one a chieftain among them"), individuals who

---

111. Joshua 2:1.

112. Joshua 2:2.

113. Numbers 13:17. *Leragel* means spying to identify the military weak spots in the defense system of a potential enemy.

would know what was needed to build a thriving nation once victory was achieved with God's help. This is an important idea—one does not send politicians to be spies! Indeed, the idea that politicians should be spies is silly. They are political leaders, and they spoke to the people as political leaders.

The people saw things differently. Perhaps they thought the open miracles that accompanied the Exodus were limited to that awesome undertaking. More likely, they still thought like enslaved people and saw the world through the fearful eyes of the downtrodden and oppressed. They wanted and thought they were to get military and political intelligence. What was the best starting point for their invasion? Which were the weakest and least well protected cities and consequently the most logical ones to attack first? And so, upon hearing the spies exclaim "We cannot attack that people, for it is stronger than we," the people "broke into loud cries, and the people wept that night."[114] Worse still, they railed against Moses and Aaron: "'If only we had died in the land of Egypt,' the whole community shouted at them, 'or if only we might die in this wilderness!'"[115]

At this point, the people even contemplated a return to Egypt. Moses did not quite know how to respond. Indeed, he felt quite overwhelmed, and all he could do was to fall on his face before the assembled masses. In contrast, God knew exactly what to do. He heard Moshe's distressed cries that he cannot lead the people on his own, and God thus instructed him to gather up seventy elders to assist him. God similarly acquiesced when the people asked Moses to send forth spies and left the final decision in the hands of Moses. Yet, now, in the face of the people's bitter weeping and unwillingness to move forward, God is far less acquiescent and forgiving. God may have been willing to follow Moses's lead, so to speak, and step back a bit, allowing the spies' mission to proceed, but no more. He now intervenes in the most forceful of ways:

---

114. Numbers 14:1.
115. Numbers 14:2.

Moses's Leadership Roles Prior to Korah's Rebellion

> None of those involved—who have seen My Presence and the signs that I have performed in Egypt and in the wilderness, and who have tried Me these many times and have disobeyed Me—shall see the land that I promised on oath to their fathers; none of those who spurn Me shall see it.[116]

Clearly, Moses's well-intended plan is premature. What could have been or even should have been the next step towards self-determination instead results in a forty-year trek through the wilderness and the passing of an entire generation. In hindsight, we, the readers of this story, realize that both were necessary for the people to grow beyond their dependence on an absolute ruler and to learn to govern themselves. Both were also necessary for the people to learn that processes are as important as outcomes, but these lessons are not so easily grasped, as we shall see.

"NOW KORAH . . . BETOOK HIMSELF . . . TO RISE UP AGAINST MOSES"

Our next story, Korah's rebellion against Moses, is further proof that Moses had badly overestimated the people's readiness for increased self-governance.

A simple reading of the text here underscores the connection between the incident of the spies and Korah's rebellion. However, let us first consider the motivations of each of the rebels themselves as explained in the rabbinic tradition before we examine the timeline of events.

The consensus among the commentators is that Korah was driven by jealousy. He was angry that Moses appointed Elizaphan (and not him) to be the leader of the priestly Kohath family.[117] He

---

116. Numbers 14:22–23. Joshua and Caleb, who were among the twelve spies and argued publicly against the "evil report of the other ten, were excluded from this decree.

117. Rashi explains the cause of Korah's jealousy as follows: He was envious of the princely dignity held by Elzaphan the son of Uziel (Midrash Tanchuma, Korach 1) whom Moses had appointed prince over the sons of Kohath

was also jealous of Aaron, as we see from Moses's rejoinder to Korah: "Now that [God] has advanced you and all your fellow Levites with you, do you seek the priesthood too?"[118]

Next among the rebels are Dathan and Abiram, sons of Eliab. There is much discussion of these two in the rabbinic literature. One view states that they served as overseers of the Hebrew slaves in Egypt. Overseers were required to report the work done each day to the Egyptian taskmasters. When the work reported did not meet the standards of the taskmasters, many of the overseers took responsibility for the shortfalls and were whipped in place of the enslaved workers. Not Dathan and Abiram. They never stepped up to protect their charges. Another view holds that it was Dathan and Abiram who informed Pharaoh that Moses rose up in defense of a Hebrew slave and killed an Egyptian taskmaster. Others believe that they were instrumental in riling up the people in the incident with the quails. Still others simply see them as a constant thorn in Moses's side, as evidenced by their response to Moses's request that they come meet with him during Korah's rebellion: "Is it not enough that you brought us from a land flowing with milk and honey to have us die in the wilderness, that you would also lord it over us?"[119]

Then there was On son of Peleth, a member of the tribe of Reuben. Many from this tribe joined Korah's rebellion, either due to the fact they had lost the right as descendants of Jacob's first-born son to serve in the Tabernacle or simply because they encamped in close proximity to Korah and were influenced by his tirades against Moses.

---

although this was by the express command of God (Numbers 3:30). Korah argued thus: "My father and his brothers were four in number—as it is said (Exodus 6:18), 'and the sons of Kohath were [Amram and Izhar and Hebron and Uziel]'.—As to Amram, the eldest, his two sons have themselves assumed high dignity, one as king and the other as High Priest; who is entitled to receive the second (the rank next to it)? Is it not 'I' who am the son of Izhar, who was the second to Amram amongst the brothers? And yet he has appointed as prince the son of his (Amram's) brother who was the youngest of all of them! I hereby protest against him and will undo his decision."

118. Numbers 16:10.
119. Numbers 16:13.

MOSES'S LEADERSHIP ROLES PRIOR TO KORAH'S REBELLION

Perhaps their personal gripes would have been sufficient to entice these men to rebel. Nonetheless, one cannot overlook the timing of their rebellion. For most of their years of wandering, the Jewish people found themselves in an area generally known as the Sinai wilderness, which may or may not cover today's Sinai desert. Regardless of its exact physical location, while the Jews were in the Sinai wilderness, no evil befell them. Even after the incident of the golden calf, which involved what many consider the most egregious sin committed during their forty years in the wilderness, relatively few were punished: a total of 3,000 people were killed by members of the tribe of Levi who responded to Moses's call for volunteers to assist in these killings. The rest of the Jewish people were saved by the prayers Moses offered "when [he] lay prostrate before Hashem those forty days and forty nights."[120] As Nachmanides, one of the greatest of the medieval commentators, describes this period: "They loved Moses as [they loved] themselves, and they obeyed him, so that had anybody rebelled against Moses at that time, the people would have stoned him."[121] Korah had no choice but to swallow his jealousy, especially when Aaron was appointed High Priest.

---

120. Deuteronomy 9:25.
121. See his commentary on Numbers 16:1.

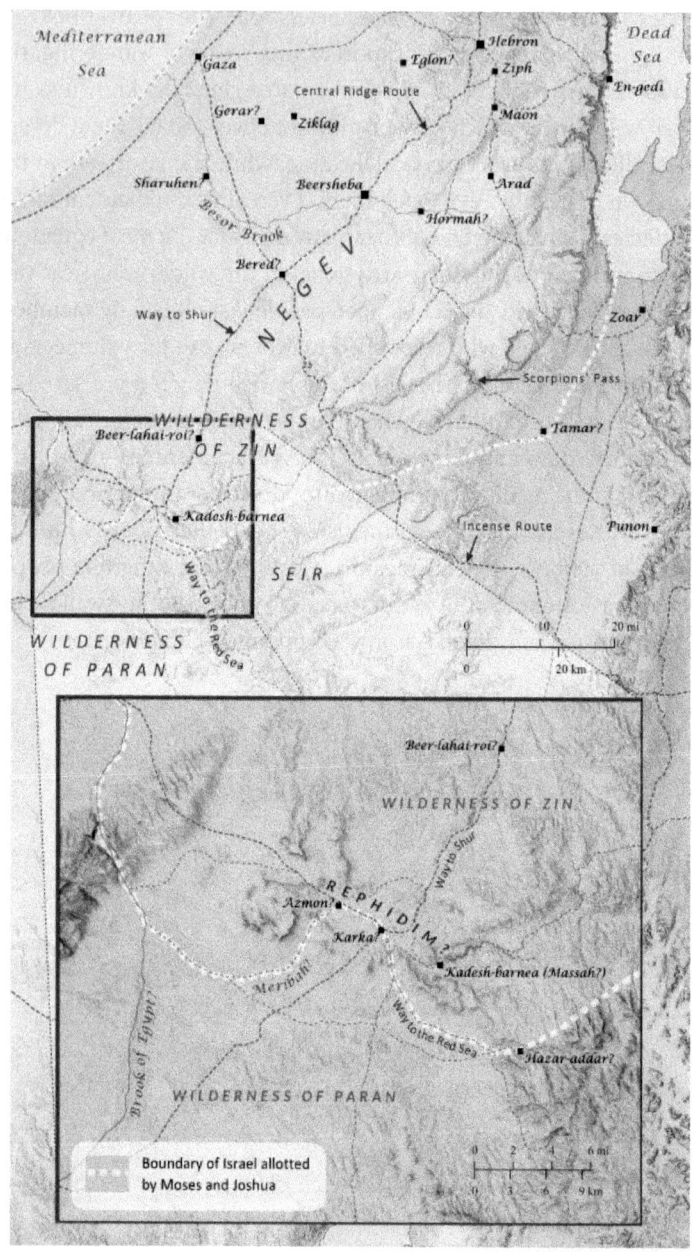

Moses's Leadership Roles Prior to Korah's Rebellion

Things took a dramatic turn when the Jews come to the wilderness of Paran which is identified by some modern scholars with the high limestone plateau of Ettih, stretching from the Southwest of the Dead Sea to Sinai along the west side of the Arabah.[122] At Taberah, the people complained bitterly and in an unprovoked manner against God, who, in His anger, sent a fire among them, which ravaged the outskirts of their encampment.[123] Many more died in the plague God sent in response to the people's demands for meat. Then there was the incident with the spies, when Moses did not pray on their behalf and the decree that they wander in the wilderness for forty years was not annulled. As a result, the mood of the people changed. They became embittered, and many blamed Moses for these mishaps. Korah now sensed an opening, and he seized it. He was prepared to challenge Moses's leadership and openly mocked him, as described by the Midrash:

> Korah said to Moses, "In the case of a prayer shawl (*tallit*) which is all blue, what is the rule about it being exempt from [having] the tassel?" Moses said to him, "[Such a prayer shawl] is required to have the tassels." Korah said to him, "Would not a prayer shawl which is all blue exempt itself, when four [blue] threads exempt it? In the case of a house which is full of [scriptural] books, what is the rule about it being exempt it from [having] the mezuzah (which contains only two passages of scripture)?" [Moses] said to him, "[Such a house] is required to have the mezuzah." [Korah] said to him, "Since the whole Torah has two hundred and seventy-five *parashiot* in it and they do not exempt the house [from having the mezuzah], would the two *parashiot* which are in the mezuzah exempt the house?" [He also] said to him, "These are things about which you have not been commanded. Rather you are inventing them [by taking them] out of your own heart."[124]

---

122. This information and the map that accompanies it are found at https://bibleatlas.org/full/wilderness_of_paran.htm.

123. See above our discussion of this incident as described in Numbers 11:1–3.

124. Midrash Tanchuma, Korach 2.

This mocking, coupled with these mishaps, led two hundred and fifty "chieftains of the community" to join Korah's rebellion.[125] Not surprisingly, Moses is more than shocked and exasperated. He is angry and shows little interest in advancing any form of self-governance:

> Moses said further to Korah, "Hear me, sons of Levi. Is it not enough for you that the God of Israel has set you apart from the community of Israel and given you direct access, to perform the duties of Hashem's Tabernacle and to minister to the community and serve them? Now that [God] has advanced you and all your fellow Levites with you, do you seek the priesthood too? Truly, it is against Hashem that you and all your company have banded together. For who is Aaron that you should rail against him?"[126]

God, too, is angry and no longer interested in supporting Moses's leadership agenda by "stepping back." God tells Moses and Aaron to move away from the community so that He may "annihilate them in an instant!"[127] Moses demurs and instead pleads with God to spare the greater community. However, Moses is in no way inclined to ask God to be merciful with the rebels themselves:

> And Moses said, "By this you shall know that it was Hashem who sent me to do all these things; that they are not of my own devising: if these people's death is that of all humankind, if their lot is humankind's common fate, it was not Hashem who sent me. But if Hashem brings about something unheard-of, so that the ground opens its mouth and swallows them up with all that belongs to them, and they go down alive into Sheol, you shall know that those involved have spurned Hashem."[128]

God accedes to Moses's prayer, as the text tells us:

---

125. Numbers 16:2.
126. Numbers 16: 8–11.
127. Numbers 16:21.
128. Numbers 16:28–30.

Moses's Leadership Roles Prior to Korah's Rebellion

> Scarcely had he [Moses] finished speaking all these words when the ground under them burst asunder, and the earth opened its mouth and swallowed them up with their households, all Korah's people and all their possessions. They went down alive into Sheol, with all that belonged to them; the earth closed over them and they vanished from the midst of the congregation.[129]

This is a tragic story and an enduring one. The Talmud relates a story involving Rabbah Bar Bar Chana who lived in second half of the third century CE and who meets a certain Arab while traveling in a desert:

> That Arab also said to me, "Come, and I will show you the men of Korah who were swallowed by the earth. "I went and saw two cracks in the ground, out of which smoke was rising. I then took fleeces of wool, dipped them in water, stuck them on the tip of a spear, and lowered it into one of the cracks. When I pulled the spear out, the fleeces were singed. The Arab then said to me, "Listen closely. What do you hear?" I heard the men of Korah crying out, 'Moses and his Torah are truth, and we are liars.' The Arab said to me, "Every thirty days, Gehenna, turning them around like meat in a stew pot, returns them here, and they cry out, 'Moses and his Torah are truth, and we are liars.'"[130]

Despite the anger he displays during his encounters with Korah and his followers, Moses does not abandon his desire to foster a greater level of self-governance among the Jewish people. He simply realizes that it will take much more time than he originally anticipated.

---

129. Numbers 16:31–33.
130. Talmud Bavli Bava Batra 73b–74a.

Chapter Five

Moses's Leadership Roles After Korah's Rebellion

As WE HAVE NOTED, Korah's rebellion forces Moses to rethink his methods and timetable for moving the Jewish people towards a model of self-governance. among the Jewish people. The narratives we found in Numbers after this rebellion illustrate the difficulties Moses faced and the patience he demonstrated in working towards his ultimate goal.

"BALAK SON OF ZIPPOR SAW ALL THAT ISRAEL HAD DONE TO THE AMORITES"

Our primary focus may be on Moses's evolving leadership role, but ultimately, the leadership of the Jewish people, be it by a single individual or a more decentralized model of governance, must meet with God's approval. Therefore, the stories we have considered so far have touched upon the roles played by God and Moses in each, with Moses seeking to divest himself of some power and God agreeing. However, there are important stories in Numbers in which Moses has no part. In these stories, God Himself is fully

Moses's Leadership Roles After Korah's Rebellion

at the helm. The narrative of Balak and Balaam, which begins in chapter twenty-two and continues through chapter twenty-four, is among the most prominent of these.

Our story first introduces us to Balak, the king of Moab. Balak himself is an accomplished warrior. In the Jewish mystical tradition, he is also portrayed as a great magician and scholar.[1] Still, he fears for his country, as the Jewish people (with their more numerous military) are on his border, having recently defeated the armies of two powerful kings, Sihon and Og. He is concerned that Moab will be their next conquest as they proceed on the way to Canaan, and he realizes that armed conflict was not a viable option.[2]

At this point, Balak turns to Balaam son of Beor who dwells in the land of Pethor. He was a well-known prophet, considered even in Jewish sources to be the Moses's equal.[3] Indeed, there were areas in which Balaam's prophetic prowess even exceeded that of Moses:

> Moses did not know when the Holy One blessed be He would speak with him, but Balaam would know when the Holy One blessed be He would speak with him, as it is stated: "He knows the knowledge of the Most High"

---

1. The Zohar (III: 184b) notes that the Torah refers to him as "Balak, the son of Tzipor" because of his wisdom and because he performed magic using a certain bird [the Hebrew for bird and the name of Balak's father, *tzipor*, are identical].

2. Balak was obviously unaware that God had commanded Moses: "Do not harass the Moabites or provoke them to war. For I will not give you any of their land as a possession" (Deuteronomy 2:9). Moreover, Balak should have understood that the Jews had no territorial aspirations vis-à-vis Moab, since they sent him peace offerings [as recounted in Judges 11:17]. For these reasons, many Jewish sources see both Balak and Balaam as driven simply by their hatred of the Jewish people.

3. Why, asks the Midrash, would God send a prophet as great as Moses to the other nations of the world? The answer is simple. The Torah states (Deuteronomy 34:10) that there shall never again arise in Israel a prophet like Moses. The Midrash, expounding one why the verse emphasizes "in Israel" notes: "in Israel one has not arisen, but among the nations of the world he has arisen, so that there will not be recourse for the nations of the world to say: Had we had a prophet like Moses, we would have worshipped the Holy One blessed be He. What prophet did they have like Moses? This was Balaam son of Beor" (Bamidbar Rabbah 20).

(Numbers 24:16). They stated a parable: It is analogous to the king's slaughterer, who knew what the king would offer on his table and knew how many expenditures the king would outlay for his table. So, Balaam would know what the Holy One blessed be He was destined to speak with him. Balaam, He would speak with him whenever he wished, as it is stated: "Fallen with open eyes" (Numbers 24:4). He would fall on his face and immediately, he was open eyed regarding what he asked.[4]

Balak had heard all these tales. He summons Balaam with a simple request: "Come then, put a curse upon this people for me, since they are too numerous for me; perhaps I can thus defeat them and drive them out of the land. For I know that whomever you bless is blessed indeed, and whomever you curse is cursed."[5]

Moses seems unaware of this plot. The Jewish people know nothing of this threat against them, but God knows, and He alone acts. He tells Balaam: "Do not go with them [the messengers sent by Balak]. You must not curse that people, for they are blessed."[6] Balaam thus declines Balak's offer, but did so in a way that seemed to leave the door open for a second, more lucrative offer. Balak thus sends a second delegation, who essentially tell Balaam to "name your price." Balaam could hardly resist, as his greed was legendary.[7] He again asks God for permission to accept this mission. God does not directly tell Balaam not to go but instead places clear parameters on what Balaam can actually do: "If the agents have come to invite you, you may go with them. But whatever I command you, that you shall do."[8]

Despite the direct "no," despite the more subtle "it would be better if you did not go," Balaam goes, but God tries one last time to dissuade him. In one of the Bible's best known and most ironic episodes, God confronts Balaam with a talking ass.

4. Bamidbar Rabbah 20.
5. Numbers 22:6.
6. Numbers 22:12.
7. Midrash Tanchuma, Balak 6.
8. Numbers 22:20.

MOSES'S LEADERSHIP ROLES AFTER KORAH'S REBELLION

In brief, God sends an angel, with drawn sword in its hand, to finally put an end to Balaam's silliness. Balaam, who describes himself as one whose eyes are open,[9] cannot see the angel, but his donkey can. She turns off the road, not once but twice, to save her rider, and Balaam angrily beats her each time. When the angel appears a third time, the donkey simply lays down. Balaam beats her with even greater anger.[10] At this point, the donkey, exasperatedly and miraculously, speaks to Balaam. The great Balaam, the man who can speak with God whenever he wishes, is reduced to having this conversation with his ass:

> "What have I done to you that you have beaten me these three times?"
>
> Balaam said to the ass, "You have made a mockery of me! If I had a sword with me, I'd kill you."
>
> The ass said to Balaam, "Look, I am the ass that you have been riding all along until this day! Have I been in the habit of doing thus to you?" And he answered, "No."
>
> Then Hashem uncovered Balaam's eyes, and he saw the messenger of Hashem standing in the way, his drawn sword in his hand; thereupon he bowed right down to the ground.[11]

Despite this humiliation, despite the angel's very clear pronouncement that "[you may] go with the men, but you must say nothing except what I tell you."[12] Balaam continues on with Balak's delegation. However, God is not through with Balaam. One greater humiliation awaits him.

---

9. Numbers 24:3.

10. The Zohar sees yet another irony to this story. It explains that Balaam's powers came from his donkey. When engaged in bestiality with his donkey, Balaam would tap into powerful, impure energies, which he would in turn use to harm people. Therefore, God's first step in thwarting and humiliating Balaam centered upon the donkey. Having the donkey turn against Balaam was the catalyst for what was to unfold, namely, God's forcing Balaam to bless the Jewish people (Likkutei Sichot, vol. 28, pp. 341–42; Zohar Balak 206b).

11. Numbers 22:28–31.

12. Numbers 22:35.

Upon his arrival in Moab, Balaam has Balak accompany him and build seven altars. On each, Balak offers up a bull and a ram in preparation for Balaam to fulfill his mission and curse the Jewish people. Balaam speaks, but only the words God allows, and these are words of blessings, not curses. Balak is furious, and he builds a second set of altars in the hope that Balaam may yet curse the Jews. Balaam speaks and utters a second set of blessings. Undeterred, Balak builds a third set of altars, and Balaam is forced to pronounce a third set of blessings.

How significant are these blessings?

One view in the rabbinic literature maintains that God wanted to reveal some of the wonderful things that the Jewish people would experience at that time but thought it important that this be revealed to the Gentile nations by their own prophet. Hence, He chose Bileam as His instrument to predict both Israel's eventual greatness and the other nations' eventual downfall at the hands of Israel during their conquest of Canaan. Realizing that one of their own had predicted all this, the Gentile nations would be even more impressed.[13] More telling perhaps is the fact that to this day, Jews recite one of Balaam's blessings each time they enter a synagogue to pray: "How fair are your tents, O Jacob, Your dwellings, O Israel!"[14]

God choosing here to act unilaterally, without the knowledge or participation of Moses, does not mean He is opposed to Moses's vision of a self-governing Jewish people. It is instead further proof that the timing had to be right for this to happen. God is a central player and not just a central idea in the book of Numbers. In Jewish law—and in American life and law—God is a central idea, but not a central player. This distinction is important.[15]

---

13. Or HaChayim on Numbers 23:5:1.

14. Numbers 24:5.

15. What we mean is that American life and culture is "God focused," from "In God we trust" on coins to "one nation under God" and so much more. Nonetheless, America does not act based on divine protection.

"THE MENFOLK PROFANED THEMSELVES BY WHORING WITH THE MOABITE WOMEN"

Although their grand scheme to curse the Jewish people failed, the machinations of Balak and Balaam against the Jews continued. They recognized that a successful military campaign was not feasible, which is why they initially conceived of the idea to harm the Jewish people via Balaam's curses. Now that that has failed, they turned their attention to the relationship between God and the Jewish people themselves. If they could somehow weaken or damage this relationship, the Jews would no longer be God's chosen people. Without that status, they would likely forfeit their rights to the land of Canaan and thus no longer pose a threat to the kingdom of Moab

How do Balak and Balaam intend to achieve this? By enticing the Jewish men to sin. And which sins in particular would advance their aims? Idol worship and lustful promiscuity, for these go against two fundamental pillars of Judaism.[16] The former diminishes the Jews' faith in God (*emunah* in Hebrew) while the latter sullies their purity and sanctity (*kedushah* in Hebrew). It is a devious plan, and it works beyond their wildest imaginations:

> While Israel was staying at Shittim, the menfolk profaned themselves by whoring with the Moabite women, who invited the menfolk to the sacrifices for their god. The menfolk partook of them and worshiped that god. Thus, Israel attached itself to Baal-peor, and Hashem was incensed with Israel.[17]

---

16. Their hatred and fear of the Jews was so great that Balaam suggested—and Balak agreed to—sending out young virgins to seduce the Jewish men. These included the daughters of royalty and nobility. In fact, the text identifies the woman killed later in the story by Phinehas as Cozbi, daughter of Zur, who was king of one of the five ancestral houses in Midian. That the men of Moab and Midian would actually do this to their daughters boggles the minds of many modern readers.

17. Numbers 25:1–3.

As for the reaction of the two main protagonists in our continuing discussions, Moses and God, the verse states explicitly that God was "incensed," but with what? The idolatry? The promiscuity? Both?

At first glance, we might assume idolatry fuels God's anger and not sexual sin. After all, the prohibitions against idol worship appear again and again throughout the Bible. There is even an entire Talmudic tractate devoted to this topic.[18] It is thus not surprising that God says to Moses: "Take all the ringleaders and have them publicly impaled before Hashem, so that Hashem's wrath may turn away from Israel."[19] Moses is quick to act, for no matter where his plans for a self-governing leadership stand, he is always primed to defend the glory and the honor of God. This, too, is reflected in our story: So, Moses said to Israel's officials, "Each of you slay those of his men who attached themselves to Baal-peor."[20] According to the Talmud,[21] the resulting death toll was 176,000! That's a LOT of people.

Nonetheless, while God may countenance the execution of many, many people, He does not threaten to wipe out the entire nation in response to their idol worship. He only does so in response to the lustful promiscuity of the Jewish men.[22] Why this is so greatly debated in the rabbinic tradition, but the resolution to this question is not germane to (and, quite frankly, beyond the scope of) our discussion. We are more interested in Moses's reaction to the most flagrant case of promiscuity in this story:

> Just then a certain Israelite man came and brought a Midianite woman over to his companions, in the sight of Moses and of the whole Israelite community who were weeping at the entrance of the Tent of Meeting.[23]

---

18. The tractate Avodah Zara in the Babylonian Talmud has only five chapters, but it teaches that the patriarch Abraham's tractate of Avoda Zara had four hundred chapters (Talmud Bavli Avoda Zara 14b).
19. Numbers 25:4.
20. Numbers 25:5.
21. Sanhedrin 18a.
22. Numbers 25:11.
23. Numbers 25:6.

Moses's Leadership Roles After Korah's Rebellion

From our earliest encounters with Moses, we see a man who never hesitates to act, be it slaying an Egyptian taskmaster who is beating a Hebrew slave to saving a group of women in Midian who are being threatened by the well while they tend to their father's flocks. Yet here, in the face of a very public display of forbidden sexuality, Moses is paralyzed. He may even be weeping.[24] What is the cause of his inaction?

Many different answers are found in the rabbinic literature. This "certain Israelite man" mentioned in the verse above was Zimri, leader of the tribe of Simeon. Zimri was accompanied by many men from his tribe. It may be that Moses was loathe to confront such large numbers of hostile men publicly. Another possibility is that Moses felt a need to recuse himself in this matter. Zimri and his fellow tribesmen demanded to know if foreign women (like those from Moab and Midian) were forbidden or permitted to them. How could Moses say they were forbidden when he himself had married Jethro's daughter, a Midianite woman? Others suggest that Moses did not know (or had forgotten) the parameters of the law in this matter.[25]

We want to suggest a completely different reason. As we have noted, Moses never hesitates to act when God's honor is called into question, which it was by the very large number of men who had bowed before the idol Baal-peor. In contrast, the men had defiled and profaned themselves with their sexual liaisons with the women of Moab and Midian. Yes, they had committed a very grave sin, one serious enough to move God to respond and send forth a terrible plague that kills 24,000 people. However, the men had brought this upon themselves with their actions. Perhaps, thinks Moses, it is up

---

24. It is unclear from the actual language of the verse whether it is the leaders alone who weep or whether Moses joins in with their weeping. One view maintains that the people are weeping in response to Moses's instructions to kill those who had worshipped idols (because, in many instances, it meant that they had to kill their own relatives).

25. This would explain why Moses and the leaders were all weeping. How could Moses have forgotten the law? Parenthetically, this legal question of whether a Jewish man be intimate with a Moabite woman or not itself was subject to intense debate for many generations.

to the people to make things right. Let me therefore stand aside and see if and how the people react. This, of course, represents a major step forward in the move towards self-governance.

Ultimately, one prominent figure, Phinehas son of Eleazar the priest and grandson of Aaron the high priest, acted while others could merely cry:

> Just then a certain Israelite man came and brought a Midianite woman over to his companions, in the sight of Moses and of the whole Israelite community who were weeping at the entrance of the Tent of Meeting. When Phinehas, son of Eleazar son of Aaron the priest, saw this, he left the assembly and, taking a spear in his hand, he followed the Israelite man into the chamber and stabbed both of them, the Israelite man and the woman, through the belly. Then the plague against the Israelites was checked.[26]

Reading the story in this manner shows how dramatically Moses has changed his leadership style, literally standing back and doing nothing, to see if some among the people are prepared to step forward and assume positions of leadership.

There is a second way in which we must read this story, and that is from God's perspective. God's anger arises in response to both sins. He commands Moses to execute those who worshipped Baal-peor, which he and the people promptly do. Yet, He acts on His own in response to the sinful sexual liaisons and sends a plague to punish the people. Rather than pray for the people, Moses seems inclined to resolve the legal issue at hand vis-à-vis sexual intimacy with these foreign women. Phinehas however, acts. He kills the two most prominent sinners and waits to see if God will support and validate his actions, which He does:

> Hashem spoke to Moses, saying, "Phinehas, son of Eleazar son of Aaron the priest, has turned back My wrath from the Israelites by displaying among them his passion for Me, so that I did not wipe out the Israelite people in My passion. Say, therefore, 'I grant him My pact of

---

26. Numbers 25:6–8.

friendship. It shall be for him and his descendants after him a pact of priesthood for all time, because he took impassioned action for his God, thus making expiation for the Israelites.'"[27]

In the end, God still seems supportive of Moses's evolving leadership plans. He allows Moses (with the help of others) to execute those who worshipped Baal-peor. God also seems patient enough to wait and see if someone other than Moses will act to compel Him to end the plague. However, by sending the plague, God demonstrates that He is not yet as "hands-off" as Moses.

NOW ZELOPHEHAD SON OF HEPHER HAD NO SONS, ONLY DAUGHTERS

While it might seem that there is a direct linear connection between the various stories we have considered to this point, there actually is none. Indeed, many years pass between these events. The story of the people's grumbling and the quails takes place in the Jews' first year in the wilderness. The saga of the spies takes place sometime in their second year. Korah's rebellion was shortly thereafter. Balak and Balaam only show up in year thirty-nine.

Given Numbers' relative silence about the happenings that take place in the interim between these stories, we can only speculate that Moses continues to lead the people towards self-governance. Consequently, we cannot with certainty connect the dots (as it were) between the stories the Torah shares with us. We do not know, for example, how the story of Korah might have inspired Zimri to challenge Moses. Or how Caleb's attempts to calm the people after the spies' evil report might have motivated Phinehas to act. That said, the story of the daughters of Zelophehad, which is set forth in chapter twenty-seven of Numbers, is the first we encounter in which process appears to be as important as outcome.

The text tells us that "Zelophehad son of Hepher had no sons, only daughters. The names of Zelophehad's daughters were

---

27. Numbers 25:10–13.

Mahlah, Noah, Hoglah, Milcah, and Tirzah."[28] According to the then-existing inheritance laws, only sons could be heirs. There was an understandable logic to this. While a child's status as a Jew was dependent upon its birth mother,[29] the child's tribal affiliation followed that of its father. This ensured that the father's hereditary land holding would remain a part of his tribal territory. Since Zelophehad had no sons, his land and legacy would presumably be passed on to non-family tribe members, and this troubled his daughters. These five women thus came forward and "stood before Moses, Eleazar the priest, the chieftains, and the whole assembly, at the entrance of the Tent of Meeting"[30] to make their case:

> Our father died in the wilderness. He was not one of the faction, Korah's faction, which banded together against Hashem, but died for his own sin; and he has left no sons. Let not our father's name be lost to his clan just because he had no son! Give us a holding among our father's kinsmen![31]

Unlike Korah, these women do not challenge Moses's authority. Unlike Zimri, they do not question the laws he has taught them. Rather, they have learned from Moses during their many years in the wilderness that the people can have a say in how their lives are run. They point out to Moses the inherent unfairness of the inheritance laws as currently constructed. They lay out their arguments calmly and rationally. Of course, Moses takes their query to God to ask if and how the law should be modified. Is this not what he has been striving for all these years? For the people's voices should be heard?

As He has consistently done in the past, God supports Moses's actions. He forthrightly declares that "the plea of Zelophehad's daughters is just," that is, He approves of this process. He then directs Moses: "[to] give them a hereditary holding among

---

28. Numbers 26:33.

29. Normative Jewish law in the Orthodox and Conservative movements still adhere to this standard. The Reform and Reconstructionist movements consider a child to be Jewish if either parent, father or mother, is Jewish.

30. Numbers 27:2.

31. Numbers 27:3–4.

Moses's Leadership Roles After Korah's Rebellion

their father's kinsmen; transfer their father's share to them."[32] Yet, this is not a one-time exception to the inheritance laws. Instead, God instructs Moses to institute a complete overhaul of the law, an outcome that exceeds the hopes of the daughters:

> Further, speak to the Israelite people as follows: "If a householder dies without leaving a son, you shall transfer his property to his daughter. If he has no daughter, you shall assign his property to his brothers. If he has no brothers, you shall assign his property to his father's brothers. If his father had no brothers, you shall assign his property to his nearest relative in his own clan, who shall inherit it." This shall be the law of procedure for the Israelites, in accordance with Hashem's command to Moses."[33]

What's more, God's command here marks what might be considered a complete embrace of Moses's leadership agenda, for this is the last place in the Torah where God Himself sets forth the law. He, too, seems to accept that the Jewish people are now ready to move forward and become a self-governing nation.

"THE REUBENITES AND THE GADITES OWNED CATTLE IN VERY GREAT NUMBERS"

The last story we will consider demonstrates the extent to which Moses has advanced the idea of self-governance and has elevated the importance of process.

The Jewish people are on the border of Canaan. Having defeated several neighboring kingdoms, they are poised to begin their conquest of the Holy Land. This is when a most unexpected development occurs. The leaders of the tribes of Reuben and Gad realize that the lands the Jews have just conquered along the east bank of the Jordan River, the lands of Jazer and Gilead, are well suited for cattle, and these tribes have large herds of cattle.

---

32. Numbers 27:7.
33. Numbers 27:8–11.

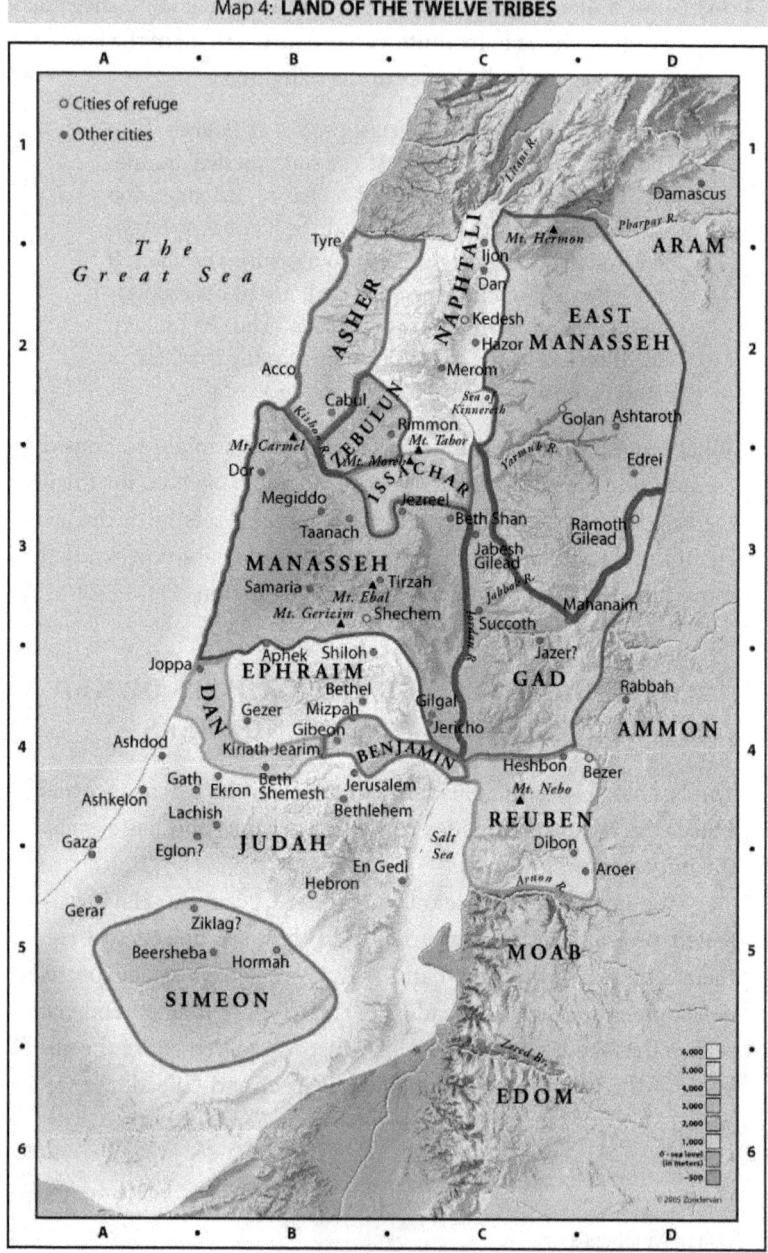

Map 4: **LAND OF THE TWELVE TRIBES**

Moses's Leadership Roles After Korah's Rebellion

These two tribal leaders come before Moses, Eleazar the priest, and the chieftains of the community with this request:

> Ataroth, Dibon, Jazer, Nimrah, Heshbon, Elealeh, Sebam, Nebo, and Beon—the land that Hashem has conquered for the community of Israel—is cattle country, and your servants have cattle. It would be a favor to us, they continued, if this land were given to your servants as a holding; do not move us across the Jordan.[34]

Have we not seen this scene before, where a small number of people are reluctant to cross over into Canaan? The evil report of only ten individuals resulted in the people en masse opting out. Now two whole tribes have raised the notion of not crossing the Jordan. Would the rest of the people follow suit? Moses immediately understands the threat this request poses. His response is quick, a bit sharp even, but without the anger that a younger Moses often displayed:

> Are your brothers to go to war while you stay here? Why will you turn the minds of the Israelites from crossing into the land that Hashem has given them? That is what your fathers did when I sent them from Kadesh-barnea to survey the land. After going up to the wadi Eshcol and surveying the land, they turned the minds of the Israelites from invading the land that Hashem had given them.[35]

There is no call for God to strike them down, neither by fire nor plague or by "something unheard of."[36] Instead, Moses enters a dialogue with these tribal leaders. Moses expresses his concern that "if you turn away from [God], who then abandons them once more in the wilderness, you will bring calamity upon all this people."[37] Unlike Korah, who was dismissive of Moses and sought to publicly embarrass him, the leaders of Reuben and Gad hear Moses's reservations. They do not challenge him or debate him. They instead acknowledge Moses's trepidation and offer a counter proposal:

---

34. Numbers 32:3–5.
35. Numbers 32:6–9.
36. Numbers 16:30.
37. Numbers 32:15.

We will build here sheepfolds for our flocks and towns for our children. And we will hasten as shock-troops in the van of the Israelites until we have established them in their home, while our children stay in the fortified towns because of the inhabitants of the land. We will not return to our homes until the Israelites—every one of them—are in possession of their portion. But we will not have a share with them in the territory beyond the Jordan, for we have received our share on the east side of the Jordan.[38]

Moses accepts their offer and informs Eleazar the priest, Joshua son of Nun, and the other tribal leaders of the terms of the deal he has agreed to. He goes on to instruct them that "if they do not cross over with you as shock-troops, they shall receive holdings among you in the land of Canaan."[39]

What we have here is a group of people who feel empowered to express their own ideas and advocate for themselves. We also have a process (Moses engaged in dialogue, not diatribes) that is as important as the outcome (the men of Reuben and Gad take part in the war to conquer Canaan). As for God, He is silent. We did not know if He is pleased or displeased with either the process or the outcome. It seems, however, that He has fully embraced this model of governance Moses has worked at for forty years. And in truth, for this model to work going forward, God must remain silent and let the people decide many important issues. He understands and seemingly acknowledges that people who do not want to go to the land of Israel cannot be forced to go. Indeed, the Bible soon thereafter provides us with a striking example of God's silence in the face of a decision reached by the people themselves, even when that decision seems contrary to His will.

It is well established from the Torah's narrative that there be a single central altar for national worship among the Jewish people. That altar, a principal feature of the *Mishkan*, was at Gilgal for seven years during the period of conquest of the land, and then

---

38. Numbers 32:16–19.
39. Numbers 32:30.

for another seven years during the period of division of the land among the tribes of Israel. Despite this, we read in Joshua that "the Reubenites, the Gadites, and the half-tribe of Manasseh built an altar opposite the land of Canaan, in the region of the Jordan, across from the Israelites."[40] Outraged, the other tribes were prepared to wage war in protest against this sinful behavior, but they opted to first send the priest Phinehas son of Eleazar to inquire further about the matter. What did Phinehas discover? That these two and a half tribes were fearful that their location on the other side of the Jordan River might at some point in the future cause the other tribes to declare: "What have you to do with the ETERNAL, the God of Israel? GOD has made the Jordan a boundary between you and us, O Reubenites and Gadites; you have no share in GOD!"[41] Their altar, although separate and distinct from the *Mishkan*, was thus not an act of rebellion but rather meant to be "a witness between you and us, and between the generations to come—that we may perform the service of GOD at Shiloh with our burnt offerings, our sacrifices, and our offerings of well-being; and that your children should not say to our children in time to come, 'You have no share in GOD.'"[42] This alternative altar was not part of the Divine plan, but Joshua honored the decision of the people, and God, with his silence, acquiesced to the decision.

POSTSCRIPT

Before moving on to examine the extent to which America's founders may have been influenced by the Numbers narrative, there are a few final points worth considering about Moses's ambitious two-fold plan: to teach the Jewish people that process can be as important as outcome and to guide them towards self-governance.

The extent to which the Jewish people came to embrace the importance of process is best illustrated by the well-known

---

40. Joshua 22:11.
41. Joshua 22:24–25.
42. Joshua 22:27.

Talmudic story of the oven of *akhnai*. A question was once raised about the legal status of an earthenware oven that had been cut widthwise into segments, with sand being placed between each and every segment. Is it no longer a complete vessel and thus not susceptible to ritual impurity, or, since it is functionally a complete oven, is it indeed susceptible to ritual impurity? Rabbi Eliezer argued that it is no longer a complete vessel and deemed it ritually pure. The Sages, based on its functionality, ruled that it was susceptible to ritual impurity.

This is where the debate and the story begin:

> After failing to convince the Rabbis logically, Rabbi Eliezer said to them: If the halakha is in accordance with my opinion, this carob tree will prove it. The carob tree was uprooted from its place one hundred cubits, and some say four hundred cubits. The Rabbis said to him: One does not cite halakhic proof from the carob tree. Rabbi Eliezer then said to them: If the halakha is in accordance with my opinion, the stream will prove it. The water in the stream turned backward and began flowing in the opposite direction. They said to him: One does not cite halakhic proof from a stream. Rabbi Eliezer then said to them: If the halakha is in accordance with my opinion, the walls of the study hall will prove it. The walls of the study hall leaned inward and began to fall. Rabbi Yehoshua scolded the walls and said to them: If Torah scholars are contending with each other in matters of halakha, what is the nature of your involvement in this dispute? The Gemara relates: The walls did not fall because of the deference due Rabbi Yehoshua, but they did not straighten because of the deference due Rabbi Eliezer, and they still remain leaning. Rabbi Eliezer then said to them: If the halakha is in accordance with my opinion, Heaven will prove it. A Divine Voice emerged from Heaven and said: Why are you differing with Rabbi Eliezer, as the halakha is in accordance with his opinion in every place that he expresses an opinion? Rabbi Yehoshua stood on his feet and said: It is written: "It is not in heaven" (Deuteronomy 30:12). The Gemara asks: What is the relevance of the phrase "It is not in heaven"

Moses's Leadership Roles After Korah's Rebellion

in this context? Rabbi Yirmeya says: Since the Torah was already given at Mount Sinai, we do not regard a Divine Voice, as You already wrote at Mount Sinai, in the Torah: "After a majority to incline" (Exodus 23:2).[43]

Factually speaking, legally speaking, Rabbi Eliezer was correct. The oven of *akhnai* was NOT a complete vessel. However, the process by which he sought to prove his point was invalid, and the Sages ruled against him. Indeed, his failure to follow proper procedure was so egregious that the Sages brought all the items previously deemed ritually pure based on Rabbi Eliezer's ruling and burned them in a fire. They then excommunicated Rabbi Eliezer![44]

And what of the second part of Moses's grand plan?

Moses went against common practice and walked away from a hereditary monarchy by appointing Joshua, not one of his sons, as his successor. Joshua took this one step further and did not appoint any successor. The days of an absolute monarch over the Jewish people had come to an end. Or had they? Some four hundred years after the death of Moses, Saul becomes king when God Himself reinstituted the monarchy. Does this mean Moses's great experiment failed?

We don't think so. The judges who came after Joshua took the notion of decentralization of power further than Moses could have imagined, but they did so in a detrimental manner. A Jewish national identify began to fade away as the people identified quite strongly (some might say, almost uniquely) with their respective tribes.[45]

---

43. Talmud Babli Bava Metzia 59b.

44. The story concludes as follows: Years after, Rabbi Natan encountered Elijah the prophet and said to him: "What did the Holy One, Blessed be He, do at that time, when Rabbi Yehoshua issued his declaration?" Elijah said to him: "The Holy One, Blessed be He, smiled and said: 'My children have triumphed over Me; My children have triumphed over Me'" (Talmud Bavli Bava Metzia 59b).

45. As we will discuss in the next chapter, the United States went through a similar phase after the Revolutionary War under the Articles of Confederation. The founders restored the country's sense of a national identity not with a strong monarch, but with an elaborate, process driven separation of powers as set forth in the US Constitution.

Ultimately, the need for the Jewish people to reforge a national identity as opposed to a tribal one led the people to opt for a king. God heard their plea and agreed to it, albeit with a foreboding caveat: "Heed their demand; but warn them solemnly and tell them about the practices of any king who will rule over them" (I Samuel 8:9). Here God implies that a Jewish king must be different from his contemporaries. Most notably, the Jewish king, unlike other rulers of his time, was obligated to follow the law. Indeed, in his all-encompassing compendium of Jewish law, the *Mishneh Torah*, Maimonides has much to say about the laws that govern a Jewish king. For instance, he writes that even the descendant of an anointed Jewish king[46] "may not be enthroned except by the High Court of seventy-one judges."[47] The king must write for himself a Torah scroll, the ultimate source of Jewish law, and always carry it with him.[48] It is true that the king enjoys great power. He may levy taxes upon the nation for his needs or for the purpose of war.[49] He may take from the nation "valiant men and men of war and employ them as soldiers for his chariot and cavalry."[50] He may take fields, olive groves, and vineyards from his subjects and give them to his servants when they go to war. The king may also allow his servants to commandeer such places if they have no other source of sustenance if he, the king, pays for what is taken.[51] However, what is often thought of as the ultimate power of a king, the ability to wage war, is restricted. A Jewish king who wishes to expand the territories he controls may only go to war with the approval of the court of seventy-one judges.[52]

    46. That is, he was "appointed only by a court of 70 elders, together with a prophet, as Joshua was appointed by Moses and his court, and as Saul and David, were appointed by Samuel of Ramah and his court." *Mishneh Torah*, Kings and Wars, 1:3

    47. *Mishneh Torah*, The Sanhedrin and the Penalties within Their Jurisdiction 5:1.

    48. *Mishneh Torah*, Kings and Wars, 3:1.
    49. *Mishneh Torah*, Kings and Wars 4:1.
    50. *Mishneh Torah*, Kings and Wars 4:2.
    51. *Mishneh Torah*, Kings and Wars 4:6.
    52. *Mishneh Torah*, Kings and Wars 5:2.

Moses's Leadership Roles After Korah's Rebellion

This may not have been the model of self-governance Moses had in mind, but it accords with Moses's vision and recognizes the importance of process as well as outcome. Kings cannot be forced upon people. Thus, Joshua appointed no one to succeed him.

Chapter Six

America's Founders and the Numbers Narrative

AMERICA'S FOUNDERS, AS WE have shown in our previous works,[1] were unquestionably influenced by the Exodus story. In a sense, it was their story, too, and it colored their vision for a nation that would embrace freedom and would commit itself to creating a law-abiding society. The founders were surely equally familiar with the Numbers narrative, but did they read the book as we have? Did they strive to emulate Moses's desire for a decentralized system of governance, one that valued process as much as outcome? Or was Numbers merely a precursor for America's model of checks and balances?[2] No matter what the answer, the similarities between the two are too great to ignore.

    1. Broyde and Travis, *Finding America in Exodus*.
    2. Whether or not Numbers influenced the thinking of America's founders, the thinker who had the greatest influence upon them, at least according to Madison, was the French political philosopher Montesquieu. As Madison wrote in Federalist No. 47: "The oracle who is always consulted and cited on this subject is the celebrated Montesquieu. If he be not the author of this invaluable precept in the science of politics, he has the merit at least of displaying and recommending it most effectually to the attention of mankind."

Moses's forty-year project in the wilderness was to steer the Jewish people away from a monarchy and towards self-governance. America needed no such guidance when it broke away from England in 1776. The founders were prepared to spell out why they would no longer brook an unreasonable and absolute king:

> When in the Course of human events, it becomes necessary for one people to dissolve the political bands which have connected them with another, and to assume among the powers of the earth, the separate and equal station to which the Laws of Nature and of Nature's God entitle them, a decent respect to the opinions of mankind requires that they should declare the causes which impel them to the separation.[3]

Virtually every American is familiar with the language that comes next: "We hold these truths to be self-evident, that all men are created equal, that they are endowed by their Creator with certain unalienable Rights, that among these are Life, Liberty and the pursuit of Happiness." Some are also familiar with that document's endorsement of self-governance. It declares forcefully that "Governments are instituted among Men, deriving their just powers from the consent of the governed." What is less well-known and less frequently studied is the Declaration's listing of the "repeated injuries and usurpations" done by King George, "all having in direct object the establishment of an absolute Tyranny over these States." This list totals twenty-seven separate grievances and includes things such as:

- He has refused his Assent to Laws, the most wholesome and necessary for the public good.

- He has refused to pass other Laws for the accommodation of large districts of people, unless those people would relinquish the right of Representation in the Legislature, a right inestimable to them and formidable to tyrants only.

---

3. Thomas Jefferson, et al., July 4, 1776, Declaration of Independence.

- He has obstructed the Administration of Justice, by refusing his Assent to Laws for establishing Judiciary powers.

- For taking away our Charters, abolishing our most valuable Laws, and altering fundamentally the Forms of our Governments.

- For suspending our own Legislatures and declaring themselves invested with power to legislate for us in all cases whatsoever.

This language makes clear that the founders had no interest in setting another absolute monarch over themselves and their fellow citizens. Indeed, the creation of religious freedom and the disestablishment of the Church of England were core American ideas—we were going to be "Godly" without God being mandatory. Thus, on November 15, 1777, the Continental Congress proposed a governing document for the new nation, the Articles of Confederation. There was a wartime urgency underlining the Articles, but the new states were fearful of central authority and extensive land claims by their fellow states. For these reasons, the Articles were not ratified until March 1, 1781. Although the Articles remained in place until 1789, when the present-day Constitution went into effect, they produced a flawed and convoluted system of government plagued by many structural weaknesses. It provided for no central leadership (that is, an executive branch), nor was there a national court system (that is, a judicial branch). Congress had no power to enforce its laws, no power to tax, and no power to regulate trade. Most damning of all was the fact that changes to the Articles required the unanimous consent of all thirteen states.

In the end, the Articles of Confederation did not create a unified nation. They did not even create a functional government. Instead, they resulted in a loose confederation of thirteen independent states, each with its own military and currency and each with its own trade policies and sometimes even tariffs.

In their naivety, the men who drafted the Articles assumed that republican virtue would lead states to carry out their duties and obey congressional decisions. Yet, in the end, the states refused to make their contributions to the central government. Its acts were "as little heeded as the cries of an oysterman."[4] Congress could not carry out such basic functions as paying interest on the public debt or paying members of the Continental army (who in turn threatened to mutiny over their lack of pay).

America during this time looked a bit like early biblical Israel of the book of Judges, when "everyone did as they pleased."[5] Similar to America prior to the ratification of our current Constitution, biblical Israel lacked a national identity. It was instead a loose confederation of twelve independent tribes, each with its own leader. The book of Judges is marked by forty-year cycles, intermittent periods of peace followed by wars. Arguably the lowest point of this era was the horrific civil war between the tribe of Benjamin and the other eleven tribes.[6]

Biblical Israel's solution to restoring its national unity was to turn to the prophet Samuel and ask for a king, a request that God grants. This was not viable for America, as the scars left by the tyrannies of King George ran too deep, and so America's leaders sought a different solution, one that we believe harkened back to Moses's push for a self-governing Jewish people and his insistence that both process and outcome matter. A rationale, if not a blueprint for this, is found in the Federalist Papers.

The Federalist Papers are a series of eighty-five essays written by Alexander Hamilton, John Jay, and James Madison between October 1787 and May 1788. The essays were published anonymously, under the pen name "Publius" in various New York state newspapers of the time. Their purpose was to convince New Yorkers to ratify the proposed United States Constitution, which was drafted in Philadelphia in the summer of 1787.

4. "Articles of Confederation."
5. Judges 17:6.
6. A simple reading of the text (chapter twenty) suggests that the rape and murder of a single woman, and the subsequent refusal to turn over the perpetrators, led to this all-out war. However, there are other reasons put forward in the rabbinic literature that maintain the tribe of Benjamin was guilty of crimes like those perpetrated in Sodom, such as general sexual debauchery and persecution of the poor and strangers, thus rendering it a corrupt debased and unjust society.

In lobbying for adoption of the Constitution over the existing Articles of Confederation, the essays explain particular provisions of the Constitution in detail. For this reason, and because Hamilton and Madison were members of the Constitutional Convention, the Federalist Papers are often used today to help interpret the intentions of those drafting the Constitution. Indeed, many scholars of the Supreme Court and many justices bestow great importance on the Federalist Papers. They maintain that the Federalist Papers provide critical evidence of original meaning and interpretation of the Constitution.[7]

Justice David Souter, in his dissent in *Printz v. United States* (1997),[8] makes this point even more strongly: "In deciding these cases, which I have found closer than anticipated, it is the Federalist that finally determines my position."[9] Justice Souter, of course, is not the only justice on the Supreme Court to emphasize deference to the Federalist Papers. Over the past several decades, many on the Supreme Court have increasingly cited the Federalist Papers in majority, concurring, and dissenting opinions. The Supreme Court has cited the Federalist in many of the most controversial cases over the past several years, including *Alden v. Maine* (1999),[10] *Clinton v. City of New York* (1998),[11] and even *Bush v. Gore* (2000).[12]

7. Corley, Howard, and Nixon, "Supreme Court and Opinion Content."

8. *Printz v. United States*, 521 U.S. 898, was a Supreme Court case in which the Court held that certain interim provisions of the Brady Handgun Violence Prevention Act violated the Tenth Amendment to the Constitution.

9. *Printz v. United States* (1997), 521 U.S. 898 at 971.

10. *Alden v. Maine*, 527 U.S. 706, was a decision by the Supreme Court about whether Congress may use its Article I powers to abrogate a state's sovereign immunity from suits in its own courts, thereby allowing citizens to sue a state in state court without the state's consent.

11. *Clinton v. City of New York*, 524 U.S. 417 (1998), was a landmark decision by the Supreme Court in which the Court held, 6–3, that the line-item veto, as granted in the Line Item Veto Act of 1996, violated the Presentment Clause of the Constitution because it impermissibly gave the President the power to unilaterally amend or repeal parts of statutes that had been duly passed by Congress.

12. Corley, Howard, and Nixon, "Supreme Court and Opinion Content," 329.

And what do the Federalist Papers have to say about process and outcomes? Consider Federalist No. 2, written by Alexander Hamilton and entitled "Other Defects of the Present Confederation." He does not use the word "process" (or lack thereof), but he certainly has this in mind:

> The United States, as now composed, have no powers to exact obedience, or punish disobedience to their resolutions, either by pecuniary mulcts, by a suspension or divestiture of privileges, or by any other constitutional mode. There is no express delegation of authority to them to use force against delinquent members; and if such a right should be ascribed to the federal head, as resulting from the nature of the social compact between the States, it must be by inference and construction, in the face of that part of the second article, by which it is declared, "that each State shall retain every power, jurisdiction, and right, not EXPRESSLY delegated to the United States in Congress assembled."

Hamilton makes a similar point in Federalist No. 15:

> Except as to the rule of appointment, the United States has an indefinite discretion to make requisitions for men and money; but they have no authority to raise either, by regulations extending to the individual citizens of America. The consequence of this is, that though in theory their resolutions concerning those objects are laws, constitutionally binding on the members of the Union, yet in practice they are mere recommendations which the States observe or disregard at their option.

Hamilton goes on in this essay to express his great frustration with the then-current state of affairs:

> There was a time when we were told that breaches, by the States, of the regulations of the federal authority were not to be expected; that a sense of common interest would preside over the conduct of the respective members and would beget a full compliance with all the constitutional requisitions of the Union. This language, at the present day, would appear as wild as a great part of what we now

hear from the same quarter will be thought, when we shall have received further lessons from that best oracle of wisdom, experience. It at all times betrayed an ignorance of the true springs by which human conduct is actuated and belied the original inducements to the establishment of civil power. Why has government been instituted at all? Because the passions of men will not conform to the dictates of reason and justice, without constraint.

As we all know, and as the Federalist Papers defend, the ultimate expression of process in the then-proposed Constitution was a system of checks and balances that is inherent in the Constitution's division of the federal government into three branches: legislative, executive, and judicial. Still, many were fearful of potential abuses of power should the federal government grow too strong. James Madison, writing in Federalist No. 47, addressed such concerns head on and dismisses them in language that echoes the vision of Moses in Numbers:

> The accumulation of all powers, legislative, executive, and judiciary, in the same hands, whether of one, a few, or many, and whether hereditary, self-appointed, or elective, may justly be pronounced the very definition of tyranny. Were the federal Constitution, therefore, really chargeable with the accumulation of power, or with a mixture of powers, having a dangerous tendency to such an accumulation, no further arguments would be necessary to inspire a universal reprobation of the system.... the preservation of liberty requires that the three great departments of power should be separate and distinct.[13]

To be clear, the men who drafted the US Constitution and argued for its ratification in the Federalist Papers understood the enormity and the novelty of their undertaking, notwithstanding our belief that Moses's vision of self-government in Numbers was a historical precursor to their actions. As Hamilton posits in Federalist No. 9:

---

13. An explanation and defense of the proper checks and balances that ought to exist between the different branches of government is set forth in Federalist No. 51.

The regular distribution of power into distinct departments; the introduction of legislative balances and checks; the institution of courts composed of judges holding their offices during good behavior; the representation of the people in the legislature by deputies of their own election: these are wholly new discoveries or have made their principal progress towards perfection in modern times. They are means, and powerful means, by which the excellences of republican government may be retained and its imperfections lessened or avoided.

History has shown how successful America's founders were in elevating the importance of process. The Constitution sets forth the responsibilities of each branch of government in careful detail. For instance, per Article I, Section 8, of the Constitution, grants Congress the power of the purse, giving it authority "To lay and collect Taxes, Duties, Imposts and Excises, to pay the Debts and provide for the common Defense and general Welfare of the United States." The process here is very clear when it comes to budgetary matters. Budgets for the federal government must originate in the House of Representatives. This requirement is so sacrosanct that the constitutionality of the Patient Protection and Affordable Care Act (ACA, aka "Obamacare") was challenged in court, with the plaintiffs alleging that the ACA violates the Origination Clause[14] of the Constitution because it is a bill for raising revenue that did not originate in the House of Representatives.[15]

Consider also the President's authority in foreign affairs. Article 2 of the Constitution gives the President the power to make treaties and appoint ambassadors. Still, treaties must be approved

---

14. The Origination Clause is found in Article I, Section 7, Clause 1, which states: "All Bills for raising Revenue shall originate in the House of Representatives; but the Senate may propose or concur with Amendments as on other Bills."

15. The Supreme Court ultimately upheld the constitutionality of the ACA, ruling in *National Federation of Independent Business v. Sebelius*, 567 U.S. 519 (2012), that the individual mandate to buy health insurance as a constitutional exercise of Congress's power under the Taxing and Spending Clause (taxing power).

by a two-thirds vote of the Senate. Ambassadorial appointments require consent of a simple majority of the Senate.

Presidents also rely on other clauses to support their foreign policy actions, particularly those that bestow "executive power" and the role of "commander in chief of the army and navy" on the office. From this language springs a wide array of associated or "implied" powers. For example, from the explicit power to appoint and receive ambassadors flows the implicit authority to recognize foreign governments and conduct diplomacy with other countries generally. From the commander-in-chief clause flow powers to use military force and collect foreign intelligence.[16] Yet, for all this power, notwithstanding the fact that he or she may be commander-in-chief of the military, the President cannot declare war. That is the sole purview of the Congress.

Even when a given outcome seems so obvious and is well supported by the government and the public, the processes built into the Constitution must be respected. Take the flag burning incident that took place in Texas in 1984. That year, an activist named Gregory Lee Johnson was convicted for burning an American flag during a protest outside the 1984 Republican National Convention in Dallas, Texas. He was fined $2,000 and sentenced to one year in jail in accordance with Texas law.

Johnson appealed his conviction all the way to the Texas Supreme Court. He lost each and every appeal until the Supreme Court agreed to hear his case. In a landmark decision, the Court declared that burning an American flag was protected speech under the First Amendment, holding that doing so is both symbolic and political speech.[17] Many were outraged by this decision, including members of Congress and then-president George H.W. Bush. President Bush strongly and publicly declared that "support for the First Amendment need not extend to desecration of the American flag." He called for a constitutional amendment to prohibit such protest, stating: "Flag burning is wrong. . . . As President, I will uphold our precious right to dissent, but burning the flag goes too

---

16. Masters, "U.S. Foreign Policy Powers."
17. *Texas v. Johnson*, 491 U.S. 397 (1989).

far, and I want to see that matter remedied."[18] Congress heeded the President's words and overwhelmingly passed the Flag Protection Act of 1989 which gave Congress the right to enact statutes criminalizing the burning or desecration of the flag in public protest.

This was an outcome favored by huge majorities. The question of the day seemed to be: How dare we as a people allow our national symbol to be so callously desecrated? Polling at the time indicated that only 28 percent of the public agreed with the Court that flag burning should be unconstitutional, and 71 percent favored a constitutional amendment to prohibit flag burning. Reaction among political elites was similarly intense and one-sided. The legislation passed the Senate by a vote of 91 to 9. The House vote was 387 Yeas versus 16 Nays.

In the end, however, process triumphed.

Once the Supreme Court rules on an issue, its decision is the law of the land, and it can only be countermanded in one of two ways. The Court may reverse itself, as it famously did in *Dobbs v. Jackson Women's Health Organization*,[19] a decision that overturned *Roe v. Wade*[20] and concluded that the Constitution does not protect the right to an abortion. Alternatively, Congress can amend the Constitution and establish the law contrary to the Court's decision.

With this issue of flag burning, Congress attempted to circumvent the process, choosing to simply pass a law that banned the burning of an American flag. Not surprisingly, lawsuits were filed challenging the act, and these again made their way to the Supreme Court. In a 5–4 decision (the same margin that held that flag burning was a protected form of free speech), the Court struck down the 1989 act on the grounds that the government's interest in preserving the flag as a symbol did not outweigh an individual's First Amendment right to desecrate the flag in protest.[21]

18. Gerstenzang, "Bush Asks Ban on Flag Desecration."
19. *Dobbs v. Jackson Women's Health Organization*, 597 U.S. 215 (2022).
20. *Roe v. Wade*, 410 U.S. 113 (1973).
21. *United States v. Eichman*, 496 U.S. 310 (1990).

It is unlikely that either the litigants or the Justices in this case consulted the book of Numbers when crafting their legal arguments. Nonetheless, the final decision, one that placed process above even a strongly supported outcome, was consistent with our read of Numbers.

What about self-governance, the second pillar of the leadership model Moses envisioned for the Jewish people? How did America's founders address this? How successful were they in their attempts to incorporate this into the Constitution?

Among the first calls for American self-governance was Thomas Jefferson's famous formulation in the Declaration of Independence: "We hold these truths to be self-evident, that all men are created equal, that they are endowed by their Creator with certain unalienable Rights." Those who choose to read this phrase metaphorically or aspirationally argue that Jefferson here was referring to the American colonists, *as a people*, who had the same rights of self-government as other peoples and hence could declare independence, create new governments, and assume their "separate and equal station" among other nations.[22]

In a very real sense, however, "all men" meant white males, aged seventeen or older, who owned land. This phrase also excluded the common people, as well as the poor and uneducated, regardless of race. America's founders were among the wealthiest people in the Colonies when they drafted and signed the Constitution. Not surprisingly, they expected the richest and the wealthiest to continue to guide the nation. Federalist No. 68 is not subtle at all in this regard, stating that the election process set forth in the proposed Constitution "affords a moral certainty that the office of President will never fall to the lot of any man who is not in an eminent degree endowed with the requisite qualifications." As Andrew Wehrman[23] explains: "[America] was never meant to be a sort of

---

22. Rakove, "When Thomas Jefferson Penned."

23. Andrew M. Wehrman is an associate professor of history at Central Michigan University. A winner of the Walter Muir Whitehill Prize in Early American History, his writing has appeared in *The New England Quarterly*, *The Boston Globe*, and *The Washington Post*.

direct democracy, where all Americans would get to cast a ballot on all issues. The vote itself, they [the founders] thought, ought to be reserved for people of wealth and education."[24]

Let us not forget that the framers of the Constitution saw to it that only one part of one branch of the federal government, the House of Representatives, is popularly elected by the people. The Electoral College chooses the president, the commander-in-chief selects the Supreme Court justices and, originally, senators were selected by state legislatures.[25] Indeed, it was only after the 1913 ratification of the 17th Amendment that US senators were elected by direct popular vote!

As for women, they were only definitively granted the right to vote in 1920 when the 19th amendment was ratified. This, of course, was preceded by many years of struggle by women who collectively became known as "Suffragists." Historians often trace the beginnings of this fight to the Seneca Falls Convention of 1848.[26] It was there that women's rights activist Elizabeth Cady Stanton made her first public speech, one that provided a framework with which to understand the purpose and goals of the Seneca Falls gathering:

> We are assembled to protest against a form of government, existing without the consent of the governed—to declare our right to be free as man is free, to be represented in the government which we are taxed to support, to have such disgraceful laws as give man the power to chastise and imprison his wife, to take the wages which she earns, the property which she inherits, and, in case of separation, the children of her love; laws test against such unjust laws as these that we are assembled today, and to have them, if possible, forever erased from our

24. Cited in Mekouar, "Today's Democracy."
25. Mekouar, "Today's Democracy."
26. We dare not forget the famous missive sent by Abigail Adams to her husband John in March 1776 while he was participating in the Continental Congress that would produce the Declaration of Independence: "I long to hear that you have declared an independancy—and by the way in the new Code of Laws which I suppose it will be necessary for you to make I desire you would Remember the Ladies, and be more generous and favourable to them than your ancestors."

statute-books, deeming them as a shame and a disgrace to a Christian republic in the nineteenth century...[27]

Does it not seem that this speech harkens back to Numbers where the daughters of Zelophehad argue for an inheritance right they believe ought to be theirs?

In one of the great ironies of American history, Black males were given the right to vote, at least on paper, long before women, with the ratification of the 15th amendment in 1870.[28] Practically speaking, however, Blacks could not freely exercise their right to vote, especially in the South, until the passage of the Voting Rights Act in 1965.[29] This landmark piece of legislation was the culmination of many years of legal actions (often filed by the NAACP under the leadership of Thurgood Marshall[30]) and non-violent civil protests (most prominently, but not solely led by Dr. Martin Luther King, Jr.). The struggles of the courageous men and women of the Civil Rights movement, who fought long and hard to have their voices heard and their rights respected, can also be said to reflect the Numbers narrative in which the tribes of Reuben and

---

27. "The Seneca Falls Convention."

28. The enslaved population of America's South was freed with the ratification of the Thirteenth Amendment in 1865. Despite the Amendment's clear intent to grant these newly freed individuals full citizenship rights, the Southern states balked, forcing the Congress in 1868 to pass the Fourteenth Amendment, which explicitly states: "No State shall make or enforce any law which shall abridge the privileges or immunities of citizens of the United States." Undeterred, the Southern states continued to deny blacks the right to vote, resulting in the passage of the Fifteenth Amendment.

29. This legislation outlawed literacy tests and provided for the appointment of federal examiners (with the power to register qualified citizens to vote) in those jurisdictions that were "covered" according to a formula provided in the statute.

30. Marshall first joined the NAACP in 1936, where he ultimately became director-counsel of the NAACP Legal Defense and Educational Fund Inc. In his illustrious legal career prior to becoming the first black Justice on the Supreme Court, Marshall was counsel in thirty-two civil rights cases heard by the Court. He won twenty-nine, including the historic *Brown v. Board of Education* case that struck down the "separate but equal" doctrine that had undergirded segregation laws for decades.

Gad argue that they should have a say in the designation of their tribal territories.

It is important to note that the successes of the Civil Rights movement inspired other groups to demand that their rights be respected, too. For example, feminists lobbied hard for the addition of an amendment the Civil Rights Act of 1964 that would ban sex discrimination in employment. After much debate, such a prohibition was set forth in Title VII of the Civil Rights Act. However, the effectiveness of this measure was thwarted by the Equal Employment Opportunity Commission (EEOC) when the EEOC decided that sex segregation in job advertising was permissible.[31] Within a month of that decision, a new civil rights organization was born: The National Organization for Women (NOW). At its first national conference, held in October 1966, NOW adopted a Statement of Purpose that in part read:

> We, men and women who hereby constitute ourselves as the National Organization for Women, believe that the time has come for a new movement toward true equality for all women in America, and toward a fully equal partnership of the sexes, as part of the world-wide revolution of human rights now taking place within and beyond our national borders. The purpose of NOW is to take action to bring women into full participation in the mainstream of American society now, exercising all the privileges and responsibilities thereof in truly equal partnership with men.[32]

While some argue that women in America have yet to achieve a "truly equal partnership with men," it is hard to ignore the changes in our society due to the women's movement. Divorce laws have been liberalized; employers are barred from firing pregnant women; and women's studies programs are now firmly established at

---

31. The EEOC formed in 1965 specifically to implement Title VII of the Civil Rights Act. It ruled in September 1965 that "Help Wanted—Male" and "Help Wanted—Female" advertising was legal so long as it is also stated that discrimination on the basis of sex in hiring was illegal. In 1968, the EEOC ruled that help-wanted ads specifying gender would no longer be permissible.

32. "National Organization for Women's 1966 Statement of Purpose."

colleges and universities. In fact, women now earn the majority of post-secondary degrees at every level, accounting for 62.8 percent of associate degrees, 58.5 percent of bachelor's degrees, 62.6 percent of master's degrees and 57 percent of doctoral degrees.[33] Said differently, there are now 148 women enrolled in graduate school for every 100 men.[34] Even in fields long dominated by men, women make up a majority of law school (55.7 percent) and medical students (more than 55 percent) in the United States.

Record numbers of women have run for—and have won—political office. Counting both the House of Representatives and the Senate, women account for 153 of 540 voting and nonvoting members of Congress. That represents a 59% increase from the 96 women who served in the 112th Congress a decade ago.[35]

Other groups, cognizant of the successes of both the Civil Rights and the women's movements, began seeking similar gains for themselves. While some trace the beginnings of the modern gay rights movement to a 1965 gay march held in front of Independence Hall in Philadelphia, most point to the 1969 Stonewall riots as the real turning point for the LGBTQ community.[36] Then there was the Chicano Movement, which was the largest and most widespread civil rights and empowerment movement by Mexican-descent people in the United States. It was most active between 1965 and 1975, but its origin lay with the 1965 grape strike in California's Central Valley (San Joaquin Valley) led by César Chávez, Dolores Huerta, and the farm workers who sought to establish a union for farm workers that would not only bring them

---

33. Nietzel, "Women Continue to Outpace."

34. Perry, "Women Earned the Majority of Doctoral Degrees."

35. Leppert and Desilver, "118th Congress Has a Record Number of Women."

36. On June 28, 1969, patrons of the popular Stonewall Inn in New York's Greenwich Village fought back against ongoing police raids of their neighborhood bar. The subsequent disturbances and rioting lasted six days. Stonewall is still considered a watershed moment of gay pride and has been commemorated since the 1970s with "pride marches" held every June across the United States.

America's Founders and the Numbers Narrative

much-deserved wage and benefit increases, but a sense of dignity for their labor and for themselves.[37]

Both the LGBTQ and Mexican-American communities have since carved out large and significant niches for themselves in our society. We think that their achievements, along with those of women and Black Americans, give credence to the notion that Jefferson's "all men are created equal" was and continues to be aspirational.

All this notwithstanding, it has been nearly 250 years since Jefferson penned those words. We may fairly ask, why has it taken so long for all Americans to be heard and fully vested in the self-governance we so often associated with our form of democracy? Once again, we would suggest that the book of Numbers has important lessons for us in this regard.

Moses worked for forty years to instill a foundation for self-governance in a nation consisting of twelve tribes and totaling about three million people.[38] According to US Census data, the population of the United States as of 2023 was nearly 335 million people! Given the geographic size of America and the diversity of its population, the sense of empowerment most Americans feel is remarkable. We have a say and make our voices heard every two to four years at the ballot box.[39] There may be times when we feel

---

37. Garcia, "Introduction," 1.

38. This estimate, considered plausible by many Jewish sources, was first proposed by Rabbi Yonatan ben Uziel in his Aramaic translation of the Pentateuch, which dates to the 1st century CE. In commentary on Exodus 12:37, he writes that each of the 600,000 men said to have left Egypt had (on average) five children under the age of twenty. This would mean the population consisted of 600,000 men plus 600,000 women plus 3,000,000 children, or about 4.2 million individuals (not including the elderly). However, some understand the verse to mean that the ratio everyone else to the men was five to one, yielding a population of 3.6 million. An even simpler approach is that the total population was five times the men, that is, three million. "Number of Jews at Exodus."

39. Voter turnout in the US has been trending upwards in recent years. About two-thirds (66 percent) of the voting-eligible population turned out for the 2020 presidential election—the highest rate for any national election since 1900. The 2018 election (49 percent turnout) had the highest rate for a midterm since 1914. Even the 2022 election's turnout, with a slightly lower rate of 46 percent, exceeded that of all midterm elections since 1970. Hartig, Daniller,

our voices are drowned out by large corporate giving or by various powerful lobbying groups. However, there are those, both within and outside the government, who work diligently to ensure that the masses are heard and our needs are met. This gives us hope for America's future. Perhaps we have yet to achieve the "more perfect Union" envisioned by the founders, but is it not still achievable? The Numbers narrative and the history of the Jewish people led us to say, "yes!"

Keeter, and Green, "Voter turnout, 2018–2022."

Chapter Seven

A Need to Look Back in Order to Move Forward

WE LIVE IN TROUBLING times. Polls show that only 28 percent of US adults are satisfied with the way democracy is working in the country.[1] More disturbing is the fact that 32 percent of Americans would support a form of governance led by a "strong leader" or the military, according to the poll.[2] How we got to this situation is beyond the scope of this book. What we offer instead is a modest proposal on how to move forward, one grounded in Moses's evolving leadership role and the lessons that it conveys to us.

For people of faith, the Bible is more than just a religious text. Yes, it is replete with ritual obligations and religious commandments, but it also contains maxims, teachings, and observations about the world and human nature. The Book of Proverbs is but one example. In the opening verses of the book, which are framed as advice to a youth, we find this exhortation: "My son, heed the discipline of your father, And do not forsake the instruction (*torah*)

---

1. Jones, "Record Low in U.S. Satisfied."
2. Woodward, "Nearly One-Third of Americans Support Autocracy."

of your mother."[3] Here, the word *torah* does not mean the Torah of Moses, but simply good instructions and advice that only a parent can give. Not necessarily about ritual and religion, although those, too, are matters parents wish to convey to their children, but also about being kind and considerate. About being a productive member of the community. About being a good person.

This helps explain our passion project, of which this book is a part. For years we have been working to demonstrate to secular readers that the Bible continues to have great relevance, especially in our modern times, and that it remains an important source of insight for so many aspects of our lives.

In writing about Genesis, we argued that its stories' cautionary nature continue to have relevance in an America where so many aspects of our lives (especially when it comes to personal encounters and sexual liaisons) seem to be defined by mutual consent.

The relevance of Exodus for our times seems even more obvious. Exodus, as we demonstrated, is about more than the liberation of the enslaved Hebrews from Egypt. At its core, it tells us of a people who evolve into a nation committed to creating a law-abiding society.

Despite what many people think, Leviticus is much more than a compendium of sacrificial laws. It contains important lessons about nation-building and fostering national unity. In today's "tribal" America, is there anything more pressing or relevant than fostering national unity?[4]

And now we find ourselves making a case for the relevance of Numbers.

---

3. Proverbs 1:8.

4. Academics have written at great length about the "political sectarianism" that dominates American politics today. "It's not just that people only trust or associate with their own side," says Cynthia Wang, a clinical professor of management and organizations at the Kellogg School. "It's that they're contemptuous of the other side, whom they see as 'other' and less moral—an existential threat. This rise in out-group hate is what we find so alarming." Finkel and Wang, "Political Divide in America." As another writer put it: "In today's winner-take-all political climate, it is fashionable to discuss tribalism in America as the new normal." Stout, "Look at Tribalism in America."

A Need to Look Back in Order to Move Forward

Early in their sojourns in the wilderness, Moses is the "supreme leader" of the Jews, not in any sinister, comic book sense, but as one who occupies all seats of power. He is God's oracle, the greatest of prophets. He is both lawgiver and teacher of the law. He is akin to a king and commander of the military. It must have dawned on Moses that his leadership position was little different from the rulers of great empires like Egypt or the small, tribal nations of Canaan. Yet, he surely also realized, at least this is our belief, that this leadership model was not compatible with one of Judaism's most basic tenets: free will.

The Mishna in the chapters of the Fathers (*Pirkei Avot*) puts it quite succinctly: "Everything is foreseen yet freedom of choice is granted."[5] Based on the verse in Deuteronomy 30:15 ("See, I set before you this day life and prosperity, death and adversity."), the rabbis understood this to mean that humans are free to do good or evil, to believe in God or reject Him. They recognized that man alone among God's creatures is granted free will. Their hope was that people would use their wills to keep their desires and lusts in check and thus distance themselves from their animalistic nature. And if they didn't, if they chose evil over good, would there be consequences for their actions? Of course, although the precise nature would be unknown to men and women. Yet, this changed nothing. People have a say in their own lives and their own destinies.

Knowing this, Moses had to grapple with the fact that there was a system of governance that denies people a say in how their lives are ruled and that this is fundamentally at odds with the religious freedom they enjoy. Thus, Moses slowly cedes different aspects of his once absolute authority to others. More importantly, God sees the correctness of Moses's actions, a response best summed up in God's utterance to Moses: "the plea of Zelophehad's daughters is just."

Did America's founders read the Numbers narrative as we have? Did they see Moses as a leader whose actions had relevance for them and whose leadership style was worth studying and even emulating? America's founders did not fancy themselves as

---

5. Mishna Avot, 3:15.

prophets nor did they aspire to the sweeping and near absolute power Moses wielded in the early days in the Sinai wilderness. Yet, we think it possible that they saw Moses's changing leadership style for what it was, one intended to shift power into the hands of the people. After all, many of America's founders were people of faith. Even those such as Jefferson, who had little tolerance for organized religion,[6] were well-versed in the Bible. Similarly, the influence of the book of Exodus on the early European settlers in America is well documented.[7] Nonetheless, in the face of King George's abuse of power, the founders did not need to read Numbers as we have. They knew first-hand what it meant to live lives with no say in how they were governed, and they were determined to live this way no longer. They crafted a system of government that not only gave the people a say, but one which also emphasized the importance of process and not solely outcomes.

This is such a critical point, for it marks the convergences of Moses and America's founders. Giving the people a voice is among the most important, if not the most important pillars of American democracy. It is also a principle that goes to the heart of Moses's evolving leadership style in the book of Numbers. Whether consciously or unconsciously, America's founders ultimately followed Moses's leadership model.

We have written extensively in this book about the importance of foundational documents, and now more than ever we see a need for Americans to revisit them. We believe all Americans would greatly benefit from reading (or rereading) the foundational documents of our country such as the Constitution and the Federalist Papers. They would also do well by reading the book of Numbers with an eye tuned to Moses's evolving leadership style.

And what might they glean from both?

---

6. While opposed to the institutions of organized religion, Jefferson consistently expressed his belief in God. For example, he invoked the notion of divine justice in 1782 in his opposition to slavery (*Notes on the State of Virginia*, Q.XVIII) and invoked divine Providence in his second inaugural address.

7. Broyde and Travis, *Finding America in Exodus*.

A Need to Look Back in Order to Move Forward

At the end of his life, Moses stands before a Jewish people who are not only free, but who, thanks to his leadership, are about to be responsible for their own lives in their own land as they become a sovereign people. Moses's parting words to the people, his blessings to the nation, were meant to fill the people with hope and promise as he spoke to their best selves.[8] Did not America's founders seek to do the same in the Federalist Papers and the Preamble to the Constitution?

If Americans today would read both sets of these foundational documents in this light, perhaps they would then come to acknowledge that a "tribal" America, one in which each side values little other than the outcomes they seek, is far from the "more perfect Union" our founders committed themselves to establish.

In the end, Numbers and America's foundational documents may have laid out differing solutions to the problems associated with self-governance, but they share a common underpinning, that is, ensuring that process and outcome are equally important.

---

8. Kelman-Ezrachi, "Moses' Final Blessing."

Bibliography

"A Brief History Celibacy in the Roman Church." Futurechurch.org. https://futurechurch.org/future-of-priestly-ministry/optional-celibacy/history-of-celibacy/.

"A Frank Statement to Cigarette Smokers." https://assets.tobaccofreekids.org/factsheets/0268.pdf

"Americans' Dismal Views of the Nation's Politics." Pew Research Center, September 19, 2023. https://www.pewresearch.org/politics/2023/09/19/americans-dismal-views-of-the-nations-politics/.

"Articles of Confederation." Digital History. https://www.digitalhistory.uh.edu/disp_textbook.cfm?smtID=2&psid=3225#.

Balevic, Katie. "9 US Presidents Who Faced Sex Scandals Before, During, or After Their Time in Office." *Business Insider*, April 4, 2023. https://www.businessinsider.com/us-presidents-sex-scandals-white-house-and-beyond-2023-21.

Berkun, Lauren Eichler. "Redeeming the Sotah." *Jewish Theological Seminary*, May 25, 2002. https://www.jtsa.edu/torah/redeeming-the-sotah/.

Bleich, J. David. "Survey of Recent Halakhic Literature: Rescue Dilemmas." *Tradition: A Journal of Orthodox Jewish Thought* 56:1 (2024). https://traditiononline.org/survey-of-recent-halakhic-literature-rescue-dilemmas/.

———. "Survey of Recent Halakhic Literature: Coronavirus Queries (3): Priorities in Allocation of Medical Resources." *Tradition: A Journal of Orthodox Jewish Thought* 53:4 (2021).

Brenan, Megan and Nicole Willcoxon. "Record-High 50% of Americans Rate U.S. Moral Values as 'Poor.'" Gallup, June 15, 2022. https://news.gallup.com/poll/393659/record-high-americans-rate-moral-values-poor.aspx.

Brownell, Kelly D., and Kenneth E. Warner, "The Perils of Ignoring JHistory: Big Tobacco played dirty and millions died. How similar is Big Food?" *The Milbank Quarterly* 87:1 (March 2009) 259–94.

Bibliography

Broyde, Michael J. and Reuven Travis. *Sex in the Garden: Consensual Encounters Gone Bad.* Wipf and Stock, 2019.

———. *Finding America in Exodus: A Blueprint for "A More Perfect Union" in the 21st Century.* Wipf and Stock, 2022.

"Chomer." Natnee.com. https://www.natnee.com/wiki/Chomer.

Claassen, Christopher, and Pedro C. Magalhães. "Public Support for Democracy in the United States Has Declined Generationally." *Public Opinion Quarterly* 87:3 (September 15, 2023) 719–32. doi: 10.1093/poq/nfad039.

"Consequentialism." Ethics Unwrapped. https://ethicsunwrapped.utexas.edu/glossary/consequentialism.

Corley, Pamela C., Robert M. Howard, and David C. Nixon. "The Supreme Court and Opinion Content: The Use of the Federalist Papers." *Political Research Quarterly* 58:2 (2005) 329–40. https://doi.org/10.2307/3595633.

"Decades of Lies Show Tobacco Companies Can't Be Trusted." Stop. A Global Tobacco Industry Watchdog. March 14, 2023. https://exposetobacco.org/news/tobacco-industry-lies/.

"Declaration of Helsinki." World Medical Association. https://www.wma.net/what-we-do/medical-ethics/declaration-of-helsinki/.

Domonoske, Camila. "Making Oil is More Profitable Than Saving the Planet. These Numbers Tell the Story." *NPR,* December 12, 2023. https://www.npr.org/2023/12/11/1217802769/oil-prices-exxon-mobil-green-energy-solar-wind-cop28-climate-talks/.

Driver, Julia. "The History of Utilitarianism." *The Stanford Encyclopedia of Philosophy* Archive, Winter 2022 ed., edited by Edward N. Zalta and Uri Nodelman. https://plato.stanford.edu/archives/win2022/entries/utilitarianism-history/.

Enkin, Rabbi Ari. "Tzitzis In or Out?" OU Torah. https://outorah.org/p/127424/.

Esqueda, Octavio Javier. "The Ends Never Justifies the Means." November 11, 2019. https://www.biola.edu/blogs/good-book-blog/2019/the-end-never-justifies-the-means.

Etshalom, Rabbi Yitzchak. "Rav Soloveitchik's Lecture on Leadership." Lecture given June 10, 1974. Torah.org. https://torah.org/torah-portion/mikra-5774-behaaloscha/.

"Evidence." NASA. https://science.nasa.gov/climate-change/evidence/.

"Frequency of reading the Bible among adults in the United States from 2018 to 2021." Statista. https://www.statista.com/statistics/299433/bible-readership-in-the-usa/.

Finkel, Eli and Cynthia Wang. "The Political Divide in America Goes Beyond Polarization and Tribalism." *KelloggInsight.* https://insight.kellogg.northwestern.edu/article/political-divide-america-beyond-polarization-tribalism-secularism.

Garcia, Mario T., ed. "Introduction." In *The Chicano Movement: Perspectives from the Twenty-First Century,* [page range needed]. Routledge, 2014.

Garfinkel, Stephen. "The Man Moses, the Leader Moses." In *Jewish Religious Leadership: Image and Reality,* edited by Jack Wertheimer, [page range needed]. Jewish Theological Seminary, 2004.

Bibliography

Gerstenzang, James. "Bush Asks Ban on Flag Desecration: Backs Constitutional Amendment in Wake of Supreme Court Ruling." *Los Angeles Times*, June 28, 1989. https://www.latimes.com/archives/la-xpm-1989-86-28-mn-4162-story.html.

Goldenberg, David. "Moses' Kushite Wife Was Zipporah the Midianite." TheTorah.com, 2022. https://thetorah.com/article/moses-kushite-wife-was-zipporah-the-midianite.

Goodman, Rabbi Dr. Ross. "Joseph Soloveitchik." *My Jewish Learning*. https://www.myjewishlearning.com/article/rabbi-soloveitchik/.

Grushcow, Rabbi Lisa. "Sotah: Understanding Change: Confronting a troubling biblical narrative." *My Jewish Learning*. https://www.myjewishlearning.com/article/sotah-understanding-change/.

Hartig, Hannah, Andrew Daniller, Scott Keeter, and Ted Van Green. "Voter turnout, 2018–2022." Pew Resaerch Center, July 12, 2023. https://www.pewresearch.org/politics/2023/07/12/voter-turnout-2018-2022/.

Hopkins, Jared and Andrew Scurria. "Sacklers Received as Much as $13 Billion in Profits From Purdue Pharma." *Wall Street Journal*, October 4, 2029. https://www.wsj.com/articles/sacklers-received-12-billion-to-13-billion-in-profits-from-oxycontin-maker-purdue-pharma-11570221797?mod=breakingnews.

"IPCC Sixth Assessment Report." WGI. Technical Summary. https://www.ipcc.ch/report/ar6/wg1/downloads/report/IPCC_AR6_WGI_TS.pdf.

Johnson, Robert, and Adam Cureton. "Kant's Moral Philosophy." *The Stanford Encyclopedia of Philosophy* (Fall 2024 Edition), edited by Edward N. Zalta and Uri Nodelman. https://plato.stanford.edu/archives/fall2024/entries/kant-moral/.

Jones, Jeffrey M. "Record Low in U.S. Satisfied With Way Democracy Is Working." Gallup, January 25, 2024. https://news.gallup.com/poll/548120/record-low-satisfied-democracy-working.aspx.

Kadari, Tamar. "Zipporah: Midrash and Aggadah." *Jewish Women's Archive*. https://jwa.org/encyclopedia/article/zipporah-midrash-and-aggadah.

Kelman-Ezrachi, Rabbi Naamah. "Moses' Final Blessing: The last words of the Torah." My Jewish Learning. https://www.myjewishlearning.com/article/the-final-blessing/.

Kent, Lauren. "Big Oil Companies are Spending Millions to Appear 'Green.' Their Investments Tell a Different Story, Report shows." *CNN*, September 8, 2022. https://www.cnn.com/2022/09/07/energy/big-oil-green-claims-report-climate-intl/index.html.

"Laity." NewAdvent.org. https://www.newadvent.org/cathen/08748a.htm#.

Lebovits, Moishe Dovid. "Tzitzis In Or Out?" *The Jewish Vues*. https://jewishvues.com/articles/tzitzis-in-or-out/.

Leppert, Rebecca, and Drew Desilver. "118th Congress Has a Record Number of Women." Pew Research Center, January 3, 2023. https://www.pewresearch.org/short-reads/2023/01/03/118th-congress-has-a-record-number-of-women/.

Bibliography

Lichtenstein, Mosheh. *Moses: Envoy of God, Envoy of His People.* KTAV, 2008.

Lindell, Yosef. "Was the Sotah Meant to be Innocent?" The Lehrhaus, June 9, 2022. https://thelehrhaus.com/talmud-and-halakhah/was-the-sotah-meant-to-be-innocent/#.

Lockshin, Marty. "What Do Tzitzit Represent?" TheTorah.com, 2017. https://www.thetorah.com/article/what-do-tzitzit-represent.

Machiavelli, Nicolò. *The Prince.* https://genius.com/Niccolo-machiavelli-the-prince-chapter-18-english-version-annotated.

Masters, Jonathan. "U.S. Foreign Policy Powers: Congress and the President." Council on Foreign Relations, March 2, 2017. https://www.cfr.org/backgrounder/us-foreign-policy-powers-congress-and-president#.

Mekouar, Dora. "Today's Democracy Isn't Exactly What Wealthy US Founding Fathers Envisioned." *Voice of America,* January 24, 2021. https://www.voanews.com/a/usa_all-about-america_todays-democracy-isnt-exactly-what-wealthy-us-founding-fathers-envisioned/6201097.html.

Milgrom, Jacob. *Numbers: The JPS Torah Commentary.* Jewish Publication Society, 1990.

Morgan, Edmund S. *Diary of Michael Wigglesworth 1653 1657: The Conscience of a Puritan.* Peter Smith, 1970.

Newkirk II, Vann R. "The Vanuatu Plan: How a small island nation devised what may be the best idea for arresting climate change." *The Atlantic* 1014, July/August, 15–18.

Nietzel, Michael T. "Women Continue to Outpace Men in College Enrollment and Graduation." *Forbes,* August 7, 2024. https://www.forbes.com/sites/michaeltnietzel/2024/08/07/women-continue-to-outpace-men-in-college-enrollment-and-graduation/.

"Number of Jews at Exodus." Aish.com. https://aish.com/number_of_jews_at_exodus/.

"One Man's Opinion–The Tallit's Meaning." *The Atlanta Jewish Times,* March 24, 2016. https://www.atlantajewishtimes.com/the-tallits-meaning/.

"Opioid Manufacturer Purdue Pharma Pleads Guilty to Fraud and Kickback Conspiracies." Archives: US Department of Justice. November 24, 2020 (updated February 5, 2025). https://www.justice.gov/archives/opa/pr/opioid-manufacturer-purdue-pharma-pleads-guilty-fraud-and-kickback-conspiracies.

Orth, Taylor. "Two in five Americans say a civil war is at least somewhat likely in the next decade." YouGov, August 16, 2022. https://today.yougov.com/politics/articles/43553-two-in-five-americans-civil-war-somewhat-likely.

Page, Susan. *The Matriarch: Barbara Bush and the Making of an American Dynasty.* Twelve, 2019.

Palladino, Lenore and Kristina Karlsson. "Towards Accountable Capitalism: Remaking Corporate Law Through Stakeholder Governance." Harvard Law School Forum on Corporate Governance, February 11, 2019. https://corpgov.law.harvard.edu/2019/02/11/towards-accountable-capitalism-remaking-corporate-law-through-stakeholder-governance/.

BIBLIOGRAPHY

Perry, Mark. "Women Earned the Majority of Doctoral Degrees in 2020 for the 12th Straight Year and Outnumber Men in Grad School 148 to 100." American Enterprise Institute, October 14, 2021. https://www.aei.org/carpe-diem/women-earned-the-majority-of-doctoral-degrees-in-2020-for-the-12th-straight-year-and-outnumber-men-in-grad-school-148-to-100/.

"Political misquotes: The 10 most famous things never actually said," *The Christian Science Monitor.* https://www.csmonitor.com/USA/Politics/2011/0603/Political-misquotes-The-10-most-famous-things-never-actually-said/The-ends-justify-the-means.-Niccolo-Machiavelli.

Rakove, Jack. "When Thomas Jefferson Penned 'All Men Are Created Equal,' He Did Not Mean Individual Equality, says Stanford Scholar." *StanfordReport*, July1, 2020. https://news.stanford.edu/stories/2020/07/meaning-declaration-independence-changed-time#.

"Religious Landscape Study." Pew Research Center. https://www.pewresearch.org/religious-landscape-study/.

Russell, Frank Santi. *Information Gathering in Classical Greece.* University of Michigan Press, 1999.

Ryding, Sara. "What is a Double-Blind Trial?" *News Medical Life Sciences.* https://www.news-medical.net/health/What-is-a-Double-Blind-Trial.aspx#.

Sarver, Samuel Jacob. *Effects of the Impeachment on Bill Clinton's Staff, Cabinet, Agenda, and Legacy.* https://pol.illinoisstate.edu/downloads/student-life/conferences/Sarver13.pdf.

Schneider, Stanley. "Moses in Cush: Development of the Legend." https://jbqnew.jewishbible.org/assets/Uploads/472/jbq_472_schneidercush.pdf.

"Share of Respondents in Great Britain Advising They Have a Positive or Negative Opinion of Queen Elizabeth II from 2019 to 2022." Statista. https://www.statista.com/statistics/1358323/queen-elizabeth-favorability-rating/#.

Skinner, Gideon. "Public Perceptions of the Royal Family Improve as Prince and Princess of Wales Remain the Most Popular and Over Half Believe King Charles is Doing a Good Job." Ipsos, April 2024. https://www.ipsos.com/en-uk/public-perceptions-of-royal-family-improve-prince-and-princess-of-wales-remain-most-popular-royals.

Stout, Gary. "A Look at Tribalism in America." *Observer-Reporter*, December 4, 2023. https://www.observer-reporter.com/opinion/op-eds/2023/dec/04/a-look-at-tribalism-in-america/.

Tanakh: A New Translation of the Holy Scriptures according to the Traditional Hebrew Text. Philadelphia: Jewish Publication Society, 1985.

"Tekhelet: The Mystery of the Long-Lost Biblical Blue Thread." Chabad.org. https://www.chabad.org/library/article_cdo/aid/530127/jewish/Tekhelet-The-Mystery-of-the-Long-Lost-Biblical-Blue-Thread.htm#footnote2a530127.

Thomas, August. "Tips for Students: The History of Spies with August Thomas." Davidson Institute, January 26, 2024. https://www.davidsongifted.org/gifted-blog/tips-for-students-the-history-of-spies-with-august-thomas/.

Bibliography

"Tobacco Products–United States." Statista. https://www.statista.com/outlook/cmo/tobacco-products/united-states#revenue.

"The Kingdom of Kush." *National Geographic*, 2018. https://web.archive.org/web/20200505060417/https:/www.nationalgeographic.org/media/kingdoms-kush/.

"The National Organization for Women's 1966 Statement of Purpose." National Organization for Women. https://now.org/about/history/statement-of-purpose/.

"The Toll of Tobacco in the United States." Campaign for Tobacco Free Kids, April 15, 2025. https://www.tobaccofreekids.org/problem/toll-us.

"The Seneca Falls Convention." Library of Congress. https://www.loc.gov/item/today-in-history/july-19/.

Trotsky, Leon. *Their Morals & Ours: The Marxist View of Morality.* https://socialist-alliance.org/sites/default/files/their_morals_ours.pdf.

"What Is Midrash?" My Jewish Learning. https://www.myjewishlearning.com/article/midrash-101/.

Woodward, Alex. "Nearly one-third of Americans support autocracy, poll finds." February 28, 2004. https://www.the-independent.com/news/world/americas/us-politics/pew-democracy-poll-authoritarianism-b2504148.html.

www.ingramcontent.com/pod-product-compliance
Lightning Source LLC
Chambersburg PA
CBHW071448160426
43195CB00013B/2056